TEACH IN HIGHER EDUCATION

Great Debates in Higher Education is a series of short, accessible books addressing key challenges to and issues in Higher Education, on a national and international level. These books are research informed but debate driven. They are intended to be relevant to a broad spectrum of researchers, students, and administrators in higher education, and are designed to help us unpick and assess the state of higher education systems, policies, and social and economic impacts.

Forthcoming Titles:

The Marketisation of English Higher Education: A Policy Analysis of a Risk-Based System
Colin McCaig

Cultural Journeys in Higher Education: Student Voices and Narratives
Jan Bamford and Lucy Pollard

Sexual Violence on Campus: Power-Conscious Approaches to Awareness, Prevention, and Response
Christina Linder

Higher Education, Access and Funding: The UK in International Perspective
Sheila Riddell, Sarah Minty, Elisabet Weedon, and Susan Whittaker

TEACHING EXCELLENCE IN HIGHER EDUCATION

Challenges, Changes and the Teaching Excellence Framework

Edited by

AMANDA FRENCH
School of Education and Social Work, Birmingham City University, UK

MATT O'LEARY
School of Education and Social Work, Birmingham City University, UK

With

SUE ROBSON
School of Education, Communication and Language Sciences, Newcastle University, UK

PHIL WOOD
School of Education, University of Leciester, UK

emerald PUBLISHING

United Kingdom – North America – Japan
India – Malaysia – China

Emerald Publishing Limited
Howard House, Wagon Lane, Bingley BD16 1WA, UK

First edition 2017

Reprints and permissions service
Contact: permissions@emeraldinsight.com

British Library Cataloguing in Publication Data
A catalogue record for this book is available from the British Library

ISBN: 978-1-78714-762-1 (Print)
ISBN: 978-1-78714-761-4 (Online)
ISBN: 978-1-78743-016-7 (Epub)

ISOQAR REGISTERED

ISOQAR certified Management System, awarded to Emerald for adherence to Environmental standard ISO 14001:2004.

Certificate Number 1985
ISO 14001

INVESTOR IN PEOPLE

CONTENTS

LIST OF FIGURES

LIST OF TABLES

NOTES ON CONTRIBUTORS

Amanda French is Head of Professional Development, Research and Enterprise at Birmingham City University's School of Education. She has worked in higher, further, adult education and the voluntary sector in the West Midlands for 30 years.

Matt O'Leary is Reader in Education at Birmingham City University. He has worked as a teacher, teacher educator, head of department and educational researcher in colleges, schools and universities in England, Mexico and Spain for over 25 years.

Sue Robson is Professor of Education at Newcastle University. She is a member of the Research Centre for Learning and Teaching (CfLAT) and leads the Teaching and Learning in Higher Education (HE) Research Group.

Phil Wood is Associate Professor in Education at the University of Leicester where he is the Co-Director of RISE (Research, Impact Scholarship and Enterprise). He teaches on a number of both campus-base and distance postgraduate courses, predominantly working with international students. His research interests focus on pedagogic innovation and organisational change, understood through the lens of complex theory and process philosophy.

1

INTRODUCTION

Amanda French and Matt O'Leary

It was arguably in the late 1990s and early 2000s that the notion of 'teaching excellence' became a common phrase to identify and celebrate 'high-quality' teaching in higher education institutions (HEIs). This focus on teaching excellence has led to a prolonged period where teaching has slowly grown in importance in HEIs. Key drivers for this slow development have resulted in the creation of formal frameworks for recognising 'teaching excellence', the increasing need to focus on teaching as the main income generator for some HEIs, the rise of student satisfaction data, particularly through the creation of the National Student Survey, and the organisational imperative to capture positive performance indicators around programme and module evaluations. In turn, these factors have become increasingly important due to the rise of the 'marketised' higher education (HE) system. In the transition from a civic to a market sector, establishing market position and unique selling points has become increasingly important business for HEIs in the UK.

As a result of these developments, universities have become more concerned with publicly demonstrating the teaching expertise of their academic staff with a view to increasing student recruitment for their programmes of study. Now, as part of the Higher Education and Research Bill (HERB) passed with unseemly haste in April 2017,[1] HEIs have witnessed the introduction of the Teaching Excellence Framework (TEF), heralding an era of unprecedented scrutiny and focus on the quality of teaching in England.

The concept of 'teaching excellence' has, however, all too often been shaped by political criteria which has played a pivotal role in structuring debate around it. These debates have also reflected how academic work has changed significantly in recent decades, as universities worldwide respond to globalisation, the massification of HE and the increasing demands placed upon them by their national governments. The so-called 'new public management' and neoliberalism have become powerful political drivers of a quality culture in HE across the world as governments have sought to exercise greater control over universities' activities, not least, by introducing initiatives to evaluate the quality of their 'investments' in the HE sector.

Given the complexity around the concept of teaching excellence and the concomitant difficulties in capturing it, this book seeks to offer an inter-disciplinary, evidence-informed discussion around notions of excellence in HE teaching. Each chapter adds to the existing literature on teaching excellence, much of which is characterised by an acknowledgment that teaching is a multifaceted and complex process. Moreover, throughout the book we aim to show how the term 'teaching excellence' is itself not generalisable and is continuously subject to shifts in context and through time.

Drawing on the authentic, grounded experiences of practising HE professionals, we hope this book will offer an insight into some of the specific factors relating to the pursuit of capturing excellence in the complex and wide-ranging context of HE teaching as well as considering the repercussions of TEF for those involved in learning and teaching and how this might impact institutional policy and practice. We also hope that it will act as a key stimulus for institutional and sector-wide debates and a reference point for initiatives, both personal and institutional, around the TEF and the wider agenda of teaching excellence.

NOTE

1. At the time of going to press, the Higher Education and Research Bill was passed through parliament. MPs and peers in the House of Lords agreed on a number of amendments to ensure that the bill became law before the dissolution of parliament on May 3, 2017. Whilst peers in the House of Lords were highly critical of the TEF, particularly the bronze–silver–gold medal rating system and its link to the setting of differentiated tuition fees, the government ultimately rejected the Lords amendment preventing the TEF being used to set universities' fees. A compromise of sorts was reached insomuch as ministers agreed to delay the introduction of measures linking TEF to differentiated tuition fees until 2020 by which time an independent review of the exercise's metrics would be completed.

2

CONTEXTUALISING EXCELLENCE IN HIGHER EDUCATION TEACHING: UNDERSTANDING THE POLICY LANDSCAPE

Amanda French

INTRODUCTION

Teaching Excellence as Policy Initiative

> *[...] teaching quality [...] should be among the most important factors in students' choices. Good teaching – broadly defined to include learning environments, student support, course design, career preparation and 'soft skills', as well as what happens in the lecture theatre or lab – pays dividends in terms of outcomes for students[...]. (BIS, 2016b)*

The focus on teaching excellence in Higher Education and Research Bill (HERB) is not entirely unexpected, political interest in the quality of teaching standards, as a way of helping parents and students to make informed 'choices' about which school to choose for their children, has after all, been a mainstay of governmental interventions in compulsory education for several decades. In this sense, Teaching Excellence Framework (TEF) is new only insofar as it seeks to embed in legislation a government-led quality approach to teaching in higher education (HE).

The current preoccupation with 'teaching excellence' as a political tool for change in HE has been evident not only in the government's own publications such as *Securing a sustainable future for higher education: An independent review of higher education funding and student finance* (Browne, 2010), the White Papers, *The future of higher education* (DfES, 2003), *Students at the heart of the system* (2011) and *Higher education: teaching excellence, social mobility and student choice,* and *Success as knowledge economy* (2016); the HE Act (2003) and the Green Paper *Fulfilling our potential: teaching excellence, social mobility and student choice* (2015), but also in the number of high-profile academic reviews commissioned in recent years by UK government-funded agencies like the Higher Education Association whose many publications on the subject include *Excellence in teaching and learning: a review of the literature* (Little, Locke, Parker, & Richardson, 2007) and *Considering teaching excellence in higher education: 2007–2013: A literature review since the CHERI Report 2007* (Gunn & Fisk, 2013). In addition, there have been several European and wider transnational reports, including *The professionalisation of academics as teachers in higher education. Standing Committee for Social Sciences: European Science Foundation* (Pleschová et al., 2012) and the OECD's *Quality teaching in higher education: policies and practices: An institutional management guide for higher education institutions* (Hénard & Roseveare, 2012), *Report to the European Commission: Improving the quality of teaching and learning in Europe's higher education institutions* (2013); as well as many independent academic studies (Brusoni et al., 2014; Gibbs, 2010; Skelton, 2007). Ironically, in the light of HERB and the centrality of TEF to its reforms, all these different sources point to how difficult it actually is to make a clear case for what could or does constitute teaching excellence, let alone how it might actually be used to drive up standards, reduce inequality and reduce social mobility which, are just some the issues HERB claims TEF will address.

Most recently, perhaps in order to prepare the ground for TEF, the Department for Business, Innovation and Skills (BIS) commissioned yet another literature review entitled, *Teaching quality in higher education: Literature review and qualitative research* (Greatbatch & Holland, 2016), which also carried out some primary research with students using focus groups to ask them about their opinions about and experience of teaching excellence. The resulting comprehensive, if somewhat inconclusive, report echoed many of the findings from previous reports and studies. Most significantly for this book, the BIS report concluded that teaching excellence is very difficult to define primarily because there are problems defining what teaching quality, not least because perceptions of it differ across different academic disciplines (Parpala, Lindblom-Ylänne, & Rytkönen, 2011). All of which makes it difficult to compare like with like, within and across universities (which of course, is exactly what the TEF is trying to do). Moreover, although research shows that students can and do comment negatively or positively on their experiences of teaching, the extent to which they can evaluate its relative excellence is debatable. This is not least because they normally only experience teaching as an undergraduate once, in one institution (possibly two if they do an exchange), so arguably they have little to compare that singular experience with. Whilst there is evidence that different approaches to teaching and learning and the distinctive experiences of learning that they engender could be significant, relatively little external quality auditing had been done on the impact of how diverse teaching approaches and the learning experiences they create might inform or affect students' perceptions of teaching excellence per se (Bradley, Kirby, & Madriaga, 2015). Finally, international researches into teaching quality audits have reported that they often generate additional bureaucratic burdens on staff and inhibit innovations in teaching (Goldstein, 2004). The BIS report concluded therefore that there was:

> *[…] limited research on the extent to which such [teaching quality] audits have improved quality assurance in universities. (p. 4)*

The BIS study focus groups revealed that students relied heavily on a university's general or departmental reputation as an indicator of its teaching quality before deciding where to apply to. Their sources for this kind of information were most often commercial publications such as *The Sunday Times good university guide*, (O'Leary, 2013), *The Guardian* newspaper's Online University Guide and the *Times Educational Supplement*'s special HE editions and league tables, as well as independent websites like *Which university?* and social media, especially The Student Room, Facebook and Twitter. They also cited location, UCAS KIS information on employment, institutions' own web-pages and marketing materials as well as their personal experiences of Open Day and other events. Interestingly, given the aims of the BIS report, the authors concluded that:

> *[…] teaching quality did not feature as a key issue that the students explicitly referenced as a reason for choosing where they wanted to study.* (2016)

In short, this most up-to-date literature review, commissioned by the government, revealed that there are real differences between different students in different kinds of institutions, about what quality teaching is perceived to be. Often, as the BIS report concludes, we know no more than students want:

> *[…] staff who are enthusiastic and knowledgeable about their subject, empathetic, approachable, helpful and patient, and [who] encourage students to develop their full potential.* (p. 5)

Whilst undeniably important, these difficulties to measure qualities in lecturers highlight the problem of trying to evaluate effectively the quality of teaching excellence across HEIs and the different subject areas within them. As Collini recently wrote with regard to TEF:

> *[…] how 'satisfied' students are with their teaching accounts for one part of that experience. Even then it is hard to know whether such reports give a direct indication of the quality of teaching, as opposed to issues such as workload, ease of getting high marks and so on.* (*London Review of Books*, 2016)

In addition, there appears to be very little in current research into teaching quality (and the whole TEF debate as a whole) about the potentially negative consequences of lecturers challenging students by exposing them to new ideas and encouraging intellectual risk-taking, which are all arguably distinctive features of HE learning (Barnett, 2007; Kelty & Bunten, 2017). Studies have shown that far from satisfying students, the use of innovative, challenging and/or unfamiliar teaching strategies often leaves them feeling uncomfortable and even unhappy with their learning experiences that may, in turn, affect their willingness to evaluate such learning experiences positively in the NSS (Harvey, 2005; Yorke, 2009).

The recent Higher Education Academy (HEA)/Higher Education Policy Institute Student Academic Experience Survey (Neves & Hillman, 2016) found that over one third of undergraduates in England believe their HE course represented very poor or poor value for money. The consumer organisation *Which?* in its report *A degree of value: Value for money from the student perspective*, November, 2014, similarly found that 3 in 10 students thought that their experience of HE represented poor value. However, perhaps tellingly, neither of these studies identified teaching quality specifically as a key component of respondents' dissatisfaction. In comparison, the European Commission's research (St. Aubyn, Pina, Garcia, & Pais, 2008) put British universities ahead of their competitors in Europe for research and teaching outcomes. Whilst HEFCE's (2016) own review of the NSS concluded that student satisfaction scores have 'increased steadily'.

Trying to define and then measure teaching 'excellence' (or even to determine if there is actually a lack of it as the current government maintains) is, it seems, very difficult. As the European Association for Quality Assurance in Higher Education's (ENQA) report on the *Concept of excellence in higher education* (Brusoni et al., 2014) made clear, where they had been implemented across the globe, quality assurance systems for HE were *not particularly geared to identifying or promoting excellence, but are more about setting thresholds for quality and encouraging improvement* (p. 13). However, despite these difficulties, the current government confidently, at least publically, maintain that they can address what they call the 'acute' lack of information about teaching quality in HE through TEF and the other drivers identified in HERB. The reality however may be more complex.

In parliament the debate about HERB was characterised, from the start, by vagueness from its authors and supporters and scepticism by its detractors, especially around the use of matrices in TEF. Debate over HERB consequently resulted in a protracted period of political 'ping-pong' as various amendments and challenges bounced back between the government and the Lords, which was comprehensively chronicled and debated, week by week, by the website Wonkhe (Wonkhe.com). The Lords contained a well-organised cross-party group who were keen to see HERB substantially amended, especially on its use of matrices and the proposal to link TEF rankings to tuition fees (Hansard, 2017, passim). However, the snap election, on June 9th meant that HERB passed rather unexpectedly into law on 27 April 2017 precipitating some hasty compromises. One concession agreed to by the government to get the HERB through was a commitment to review the TEF (for at least two years) before it gets linked to fees. However, most commentators believe it can only be a matter of time before poor performance in TEF will used as a way of justifying a differential fee structure for HEIs, identifying 'failing universities' and opening up the sector as discussed below. Writing in the Huffington Post blog in the week HERB was passed, Sally Hunt, General Secretary of the Universities and Colleges Union (UCU), argued that HERB, even with its watered down concessions still means the government can 'keep their long-term plans to marketise the sector firmly on track'. TEF, one can argue therefore, should be regarded as much more than a tool for measuring teaching excellence; it also has the potential to become the key vehicle for changing the face of the HE sector in Britain.

WHAT DOES THE TEF INVOLVE?

The Higher Education Funding Council in England (HEFCE) has been commissioned to implement the first TEF exercise in 2017. Under TEF regulations universities will be assessed and ranked, for the first two years at least, using statistical, 'big data' information provided through three existing matrices, identified in HERB as HEFCE data on student entry and retention, the National Student Survey (NSS) and the Destinations of Leavers from Higher Education survey (DLHE). Professor Chris Husbands, Vice-Chancellor of Sheffield Hallam University, is the first Chair of the TEF and he will lead the TEF assessment panels, which like the Research Excellence Framework (REF) panels, will be made up of selected 'experts' from across the sector. These experts will be charged with considering additional 'contextualised material' that universities have been invited to submit to illustrate and explain what is distinctive about their provision. Speaking in the *Times Higher Education*, Husbands claimed:

> *I'm confident of the high calibre of the panel members – selected by the Higher Education Funding Council for England (HEFCE) from more than 1,200 applicants – who will be making these decisions alongside me. (29 September 2016)*

These different sources of information, that is, the matrices and the contextualised information report, taken together, will be used to award each institution gold, silver or bronze TEF status.

WHAT IS THE TEF TRYING TO DO?

Opening up the Sector

The desire to 'open up' the HE sector has been a preoccupation of British government in recent years (Gibbs, 2012). For example, the 2011 White Paper aimed to create a *more dynamic sector in which popular institutions can grow and where all universities must offer a good student experience to remain competitive* (para 7). This theme was picked up and developed in the Green Paper (2015) which stipulated that the HE sector needed to respond more flexibly to the supply and demand in student numbers. This more flexible response was used by government in the 2016 White Paper as a justification for opening up the sector to new providers.

> *[...] in order to enable greater competition, we will simplify the regulatory landscape. We will create a level playing field with a single route to entry and risk-based approach to regulation. We will seek to reduce unnecessary barriers to entry, but, recognising the public interest in ensuring the quality and sustainability of the system, we will ensure quality is built into our reforms at every stage, from the way we regulate new entrants to the incentives on incumbents. For the first time, to provide assurance for students and establish a level playing field, we will create a fully comprehensive register of higher education providers. (*White paper, *2016)*

To facilitate the creation of a more 'level playing field', the government sought to create a 'comprehensive register' where HEIs are ranked through TEF. In this way, through TEF, the conceptualisation of 'teaching excellence' has been largely uncoupled from HE's more traditional liberal and democratic traditions. Instead, HEIs are increasingly positioned as key players in an international 'knowledge economy' (Ball, 2008; OECD, 2015). As ENQA report *Concepts of Excellence in Higher Education* (2014) concluded:

> *There is a perceptible shift in thinking away from utilitarian notions of equity and the view of higher education as a 'social good' towards the promotion of a more competitive market for institutions in the belief that competition will improve standards and quality. (Brusconi, 2014, p. 19)*

For students in such a marketised, competitive economy, an HE experience is primarily judged on the extent to which it can be considered 'value for money' (or not). This question of 'value for money', moreover, is almost entirely predicated on the idea that a university education increases individuals' employability and earning power, which further reinforces the idea of HE as a tiered marketplace with students located as consumers of a commodified educational product.

However, there is concern that ranking HEIs through TEF will exacerbate existing hierarchies and precipitate some institutions into collapse. For example, any organisation placed on the lowest TEF tier may find it ever harder, over time, to recruit enough students to cover their costs. Deemed 'failing universities' they may get trapped in a vicious circle where their financial difficulties, due to low recruitment or capped fees, mean that they will only be able or willing to offer stripped-down teaching on a limited number of programmes, thus increasing their chances of continuing to score badly on TEF evaluations. Moreover, in an increasingly competitive landscape universities may struggle to recruit students precisely because they have been actively encouraged to see the

TEF ratings as a blanket proxy for teaching quality. However, there are many other reasons why a university may score low on the various TEF matrices; they may specialise in vocational courses where student employment opportunities are limited or low-paid and which therefore rate less favourably on TEF matrices such as DLHE. Or they may be operating in a very fierce commercial marketplace, such as London, which is very popular with international students for geographical as much as educational reasons (Holmwood, Hickey, Cohen, & Wallis, 2016).

However, irrespective of any underlying reasons, if a university is deemed to have failed HERB will make it easier for new and alternative for-profit or private providers to enter the market. These new providers will not have to meet the current quality checks and balances required by the HEFCE, Quality Assurance Agency (QAA) and Privy Council, which are all to be replaced by new 'Office for Students' working in conjunction with the QAA. This is a worrying development and during the debates about HERB in the House of Lords peers had tried to insist that institutions wishing to become universities must develop a track record of successful delivery in HE before they could do so (Hansard, 2017, passim). Despite their concerns, HERB passed with an agreement that new providers need only convince an independent committee that they are 'good enough'. How HERB intends to sustain rigorous scrutiny and monitoring in an expanded and increasingly privatised HE sector, however, remains unclear.

The government's determination to rank existing universities through the TEF, whilst simultaneously attempting to create 'a more level field' in which new providers can more easily emerge, reinforces the view of many critics of HERB, that it is a 'Trojan horse', using TEF in particular, to mask the increased marketisation of HE (Collini, 2016;

Holmwood et al., 2016; McGettigan, 2013). The history of using matrices to measure excellence in educational settings, of one type of another, is chequered and highly contested, not least because there are particular problems associated with using matrices to measure something as nebulous as teaching excellence. Nonetheless, it is entirely predictable that matrices were the go-to assessment/evaluation tools chosen by the government for the TEF as they embody the 'New Public Management' (NPM) quality discourse, which has dominated HE globally for several decades now. Typically, NPM strategies or policies, in any setting, are mobilised as a response to arrange of economic, social, political and technological issues which are perceived to be affecting that setting. These issues inevitably coalesce around a 'crisis' of one kind or another, which necessitates restructuring in order to achieve greater efficiency and value for money (Deem, Hillyard, & Reed, 2007). Arguably, the alleged problems in HE around teaching quality could be seen as one such NPM solution-driven crisis.

Despite the popularity of NPM solutions, big data-driven target-setting and ranking remain problematic; in particular, there is often a lack of consensus about the conclusions that can be drawn from data collected on a large scale (Harfold, 2014; Tinati, Halford, Carr, & Pope, 2014). For example, it is difficult to measure 'value added' using matrices. This, of course, is why HERB includes a requirement for universities to provide additional contextualised information for the TEF. Similarly, the government were initially interested in drilling down into data about teaching quality within disciplines, across and within institutions for TEF (BIS, 2016b). However, problems defining the term 'subject' and working out how subject assessments and wider institutional TEF rating could or would combine, mean that it has not made its way into the final draft of HERB (for now at least). Finally, there is also the well-documented dangers of perverse incentives or unintended outcomes which often arise from the (mis)use of big data due to organisations over-zealously responding to, or deliberately gaming blanket target-setting of the type proposed by TEF (McCaig & Taylor, 2015; Wilsdon, 2015). For example, in early 2017 Ofsted announced that it would holding an investigation into the ways in which many schools sough to game their results to improve their place on league tables. This move was prompted, in part, by research on big data sets in UK schools from the quantitative researchers at Education Datalab (educationdatalab.org.uk). On a global scale Goldstein's (2004) research into the effects of UNESCO's 2002 'Education for All' (EFA) initiative has discussed how its emphasis on numerically driven targets to boost teaching standards resulted in countries dumbing down their curricula, teaching to the test and grade inflation.

The BIS report (Greatbatch & Holland, 2016) drew attention to the wide range of matrices currently being used for measuring teaching quality around the world. However, its authors were clear that researchers looking into teaching quality were wary of linking hard empirical data such as how much someone paid in tuition fees, the staff/student ratio in their classes, the classification of degree they came out with and how much they earned after graduation can tell anyone how satisfied students ultimately were with the whole experience of being taught at university. Despite the lack of evidence proving that data-driven metrics can be used to say something meaningful about the experience of being taught, TEF is one of the latest examples of how big data is increasingly being deployed as a tool by government to give their policies a superficially quantitative evidential basis.

TEF AND STUDENT SATISFACTION

The NSS was commissioned in 2005 by the HEFCE as part of a revised quality assurance framework with a duel function. Firstly, it was to make HEIs more accountable for the educational experience they were delivering to undergraduates and secondly it aimed to better inform university applicants about the strengths and weaknesses of respective HEIs. It goes out annually to final-year undergraduate students and in 2016, 431,000 students were invited to take part (HEFCE, 2016). TEF, continues to rely heavily on the NSS even though response rates are patchy across the sector despite the incessant bribing of students to complete it. HEFCE who now administer the NSS have just completed a review and evaluation of the survey that took over two years to complete (2016). After over 10 years of running the survey and hundreds and thousands of responses, the HEFCE survey revealed that overall satisfaction rates are now over 80% and some individual courses get 100% satisfaction.

However, since its inception the NSS has been heavily criticised which goes someway to explaining the current disquiet about its centrality to TEF. In 2008, Lee Harvey resigned as the HEA's Director of Research and Evaluation having criticised the survey as 'bland' and 'methodologically worthless' (THS, 2008). More recently, in its discussion of HERB, the House of Lords raised questions about the NSS's ability to provide useful information about teaching quality and student satisfaction across different institutions. In the early 2017, the NUS began a campaign of boycotting NSS to draw attention to TEFs limitations. Whilst the Royal Statistical Society's response to the government's *Technical consultation on the Teaching Excellence Framework* (2017) called it more of a voluntary census rather than statistical survey and argued it should not be used to determine important issues such as funding for and ranking of HEIs.

Arguably, NSS scores inevitably reveal more about each university's ability to manage the process of the NSS as it clear that most universities have worked out how to game the NSS. For example, students are pre-tested in some institutions so that they can encouraged to score more positively when they complete the actual survey. Poster campaigns and freebies promote participation in the NSS as way for students to ensure their 'voice' gets heard. Although, ironically the students who complete it will have left university long before any changes could be made on the basis of their feedback in the NSS. Worryingly, there is evidence suggesting that the NSS has certain potentially damaging in-built biases. For example, students report greater satisfaction when courses are less challenging, this has resulted in many lecturers becoming increasingly fearful of challenging students or taking them out of their comfort zone as it may result in low NSS scores. Additionally, there are studies that suggest it could reflect student bias against female and ethnic-minority lecturers as several recent studies have shown that male lecturers consistently receive higher student evaluation scores than female lecturers; even though there is no evidence that they are more effective teachers (MacNell, Driscoll, & Hunt, 2015). This holds true even when something objective is measured, like how long individual lecturers take to give feedback. Moreover, students often expect their male and female lecturers to conform to gendered behaviours and are critical of those who fail to do so (Boring, Ottoboni, & Stark, 2016).

Finally, given that all universities employ similar tactics to boost their NSS scores, there is actually relatively little variation in the data gathered. In addition, The Office of National Statistics (ONS) in its *Review of data sources for the TEF 2016* (published online June 2016) reported that in the NSS there is consistent [...] *under-reporting of certain groups and over-coverage of others [which] could lead to bias in use of the data*. However, even small differences can send an institution dropping like a stone or soaring up the ratings. It is perhaps, therefore, not too surprising that even Husbands has called the NSS the *least important* of the three main metric sources (THE, 2016).

It has been implicitly recognised by the architects of the HERB that matrices are inevitably crude ways of measuring something as nebulous and contested as teaching or excellence (as the other chapters in this book will show). However, its architects have argued that the use of benchmarking and split metrics, both established forms of management information in education (e.g. benchmarking has already been used for several years by HESA nationally and internationally to highlight similarities and differences between universities), will be used in the TEF to flag up more subtle differences, especially with regard to performance around WP/BME recruitment and retention and employability.

However, as the *Times Higher Education*'s 'mock TEF' exercise, released June 2016, rated the many of the Russell Group institutions quite low down, revealing in the process that benchmarking could create an alternative league table, based on, for example, recruitment and retention of WP students. Although the THE's mock-TEF created a flurry of indignation from the more elite institutions and their defenders, it is probable that the long-established 'prestige' associated with more elite research-intensive HEIs (and the snobbery that goes with it) will ensure that the metrics in TEF will struggle to work in any meaningful way as irrespective of scores for 'teaching quality' in HE students will chose more prestigious institutions over less prestigious ones (Blackmore, Blackwell, & Edmondson, 2016).

> *[...] social and cultural value [in higher education] is signaled by a degree and where it comes from. Parents and students understand how prestige works. (Blackmore et al., 2016)*

Furthermore, the exclusivity of many elite institutions is a key factor in their prestige, an inconvenient fact that fatally undermines the WP agenda running through TEF. Also because TEF ratings, in the first instance at least, will relate to the university, not the subject or course, courses that receive excellent feedback from students may find themselves in a poorly rating university and vice versa, making it difficult for students to make a judgement on TEF alone. The issue of assessing teaching quality and using it to help students and employers make judgements about and compare different HEIs is therefore, according to Blackmore et al. (2016) an irresolvable 'wicked issue' for the government.

TEF AND EMPLOYABILITY

Ostensibly, another important impetus for TEF is to give employers, as well as students, better information about the quality of universities across the sector. Even though BIS's own commissioned research found graduate employers were *mostly satisfied with the graduates they had hired* (Pollard et al., 2015, p. 13). Whilst the focus groups held as part of the recent BIS report *Teaching quality in higher education: Literature review and qualitative research* (2016) revealed students' scepticism about the inclusion of employment outcomes within the TEF because they felt *graduate employability is not a measure of teaching quality* (p. 48), even though they agreed that information about employment rates might be useful due to the competitiveness of the job market.

The employability main proxy used in TEF, DLHE is a survey published by HESA (www.hesa.ac.uk/data-and-analysis/students/destinations) which determines student destinations and wages six months after leaving university. However, as with the NSS there are a number of other variables, outside of teaching quality, which affect students' chances of employment and the subsequent earning power. These include the perceived standing of the university they attended, which in turn reflects entrench socio-economic differences between student cohorts in pre- and post-1992 HEIs, irrespective of the quality of the teaching students receive there (Bell & Brooks, 2016). This is evidenced by the fact that Russell Group institutions often perform far better on employment metrics like DHLE than they do on NSS as demonstrated by the THE's mock TEF in June 2015. In addition, different degrees are potentially always going to provide a better chance of employment immediately upon leaving university, for example teaching and nursing, whereas others are more likely provide access to high-paying jobs such as accountancy and law.

For future iterations of TEF the government have also suggested including other matrixes such as the Longitudinal Educations Outcome (LEO) dataset which draws on information from the National Pupil Database (NPD), the Individualised Learner Record (ILR), the Higher Education Statistics Agency (HESA), Her Majesty's Revenue and Customs data (HMRC), The National Benefit Database, the Labour Market System and Juvos, the unemployment research database. In series of experiments data releases LEO have already begin to provide a more detailed picture of students' journeys into and through HE onwards to employment. LEO data undoubtedly provides more information regarding the different employment trajectories experienced by widening participation HE students as it can differentiate across ethnicity or the different employment pattern of male and female students. It also reveals that prior attainment and socio-economic background are far bigger predictors of employment outcomes than any other factor under universities' control. The complex set of variables affecting graduate employment therefore casts doubt on the utility of DHLE as a TEF matrix.

TEF AND WP

The government's stated aim is to use TEF ratings to give 'a clear signal to students', especially those from disadvantaged backgrounds, about the best place for them to study, the relative value for money of their chosen degree and potential employment outcomes of their graduate 'choices' (BIS, 2015, p. 22). Under HERB, universities will be required to publish the gender, ethnicity and social backgrounds of their student intake to 'shine a light on their admissions processes' (HERB, 2017). Whilst the new Office for Students will be charged with promoting, not only 'access', but also 'participation', retention and graduate employment figures (BIS, 2016b).

This emphasis on WP is politically important as the current government want to double the number of people from disadvantaged backgrounds and increase the number of BME students going to HE by 20%, by 2020. This intention is reflected in HERB as universities will be required to have measures in place to facilitate the recruitment, retention and successful progression of disadvantaged groups and the success of these measures will be gauged through the TEF. As Professor Les Ebdon, Director of Fair Access to Higher Education, said in a recent government press release (September 2016).

> *[...] The links to fair access have been further strengthened, following clear support from the sector in their consultation responses. It is especially pleasing to see specific measures on positive outcomes for disadvantaged students, and clear instructions to TEF panellists that they should consider disadvantaged students at every stage.*

However, the aspiration to improve widening participation represents a real challenge as currently any analysis of the socio-economic intake of individual university student populations reveals that participation rates in HE by disadvantaged students have actually been uneven, and even inequitable, across English universities since 'massification' (Scott, 2000) resulting in very different experiences and perceptions of the sector as a whole between different social groups (Bathmaker et al., 2016). This trend appears to have become more entrenched in recent years and has been clearly linked to the increased marketisation of the sector (Leathwood, 2010; McGettigan, 2013).

Research shows that the numbers of WP students differ substantially according to the type of institution, mode of study and type and level of course undertaken (Boliver, 2011; Jones, 2010; Reay, Davies, David, & Ball, 2001; York, 2009). This is something that the White Paper (BIS, 2016b) acknowledges:

> *Although applicants from disadvantaged backgrounds are at record levels, a disproportionate number of entrants to Russell Group 13 Success as a Knowledge Economy: Teaching Excellence, Social Mobility and Student Choice universities come from a tiny minority of the country's state-funded secondary schools25. English 18 year olds from the most*

> *advantaged backgrounds were 6.3 times more likely to go to higher tariff institutions in 2015 than those from the least advantaged backgrounds26. Higher Education Funding Council for England (HEFCE) research finds that the noncontinuation rates for black students in university are much higher than for white students27, even when taking into account facts such as prior educational attainment – and success within higher education is uneven too. Disparities like these cannot be explained by prior educational attainment alone.*

Indeed, the various ways in which HE adds or detracts from any individual's social mobility and/or capital are complex and well documented. Much recent research has explored the extent to which the experiences of students, pre, during and post university are differentiated by class, irrespective of their discipline and ultimate achievement (Bathmaker et al., 2016; Boliver, 2011; Goldthorpe, 2016; Vignoles, 2013). Moreover, the work of Britton, Dearden, Shephard, and Vignoles (2016) reveals that that graduate earnings are significantly less for students from low-income families when compared to students from more affluent backgrounds, even then they have completed the same degrees from the same universities.

Research also indicates that different types of students make decisions about their choice of university based on very different criteria. Not only do they consider the reputation of an institution and the availability of courses but for many, especially mature and WP students, it is clear that proximity of work, family and friendships networks and the diversity (or lack of it) of the student body they are joining, also play an important role in decision-making (Christie, 2007).

REF AND TEF

In addition to improving the experience of students as learners, that is, as the recipients of teaching excellence or otherwise, the supporters of TEF claim it will rebalance the unequal relationship between teaching and research which has traditionally informed HE rankings, especially with regard to the pre-eminence of more elite research-intensive universities.

> *The TEF will, for the first time, link the funding of teaching in higher education to quality and not simply quantity – a principle that has long been established for research. (Jo Johnson; BIS White paper, 2016; Success as knowledge economy: Teaching excellence, social mobility and student choice)*

The historical prioritising of research, alongside the attention drawn to it through the REF, previously the RAE (introduced in 1986) has, it has been argued, focused attention away from issues around teaching and teaching excellence in HE.

> *For the first time, it (TEF) will give a clear signal to those of us in the sector that the quality of our teaching is as important as the quality of our research. (Chris Husbands,* THE, *September 2016)*

For this reason, TEF has been justified as an overdue opportunity to refocus the importance of teaching quality in universities.

> *For too long, teaching has been the poor cousin of research. Skewed incentives have led to a progressive decline in the relative status of teaching as an activity. (BIS, 2016b)*

Most academics welcome the renewed focus on teaching on HE however REF like TEF is seeking to measure something complex and multifaceted using a series of proxies. For this reason many of the criticisms levelled at TEF can be and have been levelled at REF, not least that the government need to be clear what each framework is seeking to measure. REF has mutated over the years as the government have tried to use it to manage and marketise research in HE. Although it began life as a formula to determine the allocation of research funding from central government to universities, it is now also used, implicitly and explicitly, to demonstrate accountability for that funding, measure the reputation of HEIs with regard to the research they produce and influence (through funding) the development of research cultures in HEIs across the sector. TEF, as discussed in this chapter, starts out as a multipurpose tool and may well fall foul of the same problems of the REF not least because there are fears that will do none of the jobs it has been charged with well, or well enough. Moreover, there are plenty of claims that REF has skewed the research culture of HE negatively, that it is subject to gaming and has got more and more expensive to administer. Cleary, there is plenty that the government could learn from REF with regard to the implementation of TEF, the question is are they willing to?

CONCLUDING THOUGHTS

In summary, the contestability of so many of the concepts being ostensibly measured by TEF, such as 'quality', 'excellence' and 'satisfaction', needs to inform any ongoing debate, post the passing of HERB, about the relative merits and shortcomings of all of the proposed matrices informing TEF. In addition, it will be necessary to monitor the extent to which the matrices, individually and taken together, are actually helping students, and employers form a better understanding of the quality and utility of what universities have to offer (both on their own terms and in comparison to other HEIs). As discussed above it appears probable that creating a tiered HE system, through the imposition of TEF rankings, may exacerbate existing inequalities around the status and currency of qualifications that will most definitely not benefit students from disadvantaged backgrounds (Bathmaker et al., 2016).

This is something that flies in the face of one of the stated aims of HERB, namely to promote further access to university for widening participation students. Government also has responsibility to ensure, as much as possible, against the kinds of gaming the HE sector has already experienced across the sector with the REF and the NSS (Jump, 2015; Wilsdon, 2015). Guarding against increasing bureaucracy in universities is another concern. Universities already spend around 8% of their annual teaching budgets — around £1.1bn — on various 'quality assurance' measures such as the REF, which taken together cost around £232m in 2014. Adding to this financial burden, as TEF will inevitably do, is a worry in a time of cuts and budget constraints in HE (Holmwood et al., 2016).

It is important to keep in play other possible measures for improving students' learning experience HE. These could include making additional public funding available to reverse the worsening staff-to-student ratio in many institutions and disciplines, so that staff can support students more effectively. Regulating academic staff workloads, which according to the recent UCU report *Education is a workload issue* (2016) often total over 50 hours per week. Both of these measures would also allow staff time to engage in the kinds of ongoing professional development and research activities as discussed in the following chapters, which have been proven to improve teaching and learning experiences in HE (Bradeley, Kirby, & Madriaga, 2015). There are also more qualitative ways of measuring teaching quality that recognise that teaching is an essentially complex form of social interaction, as discussed in Chapters 3 and 4.

As Collini (2016) writes in his scathing review of the Green paper (2015) *Fulfilling our potential: Teaching excellence, social mobility and student choice*

> *[...] the Green Paper doesn't know what it means by 'teaching quality'. It treats it as the equivalent or sum of a number of things that can be measured. So, if a course provides a clear description of its aims and procedures; if the number of contact hours and requirements for written work are as advertised and the work is marked and returned promptly; if few students drop out; if students on the course have had a good record of subsequent employment; and if many students say they were 'satisfied' or 'very satisfied' with the course – then all that is taken as proof that high-quality teaching has taken place. (p. 35)*

A failure to engage with the complexity of teaching excellence is one of the main reasons TEF has generated a huge amount of controversy within and outside of HE. Indeed, one can argue that recognising the essential complexity of teaching may be better served by HEIs developing the kind of communities of teaching practice discussed elsewhere in this book.

However, TEF is here to stay for the foreseeable future and it will inevitably remain a source of much anxiety for lecturers and managers alike, as the stakes for each university are so high, irrespective of the fact that it will play out in different ways for different HEIs. Elite universities may continue to struggle to recruit WP students and NSS scores will no doubt cause assorted problems for courses and disciplines across the sector, for a variety of reasons that may or may not be the consequence of poor teaching. Employability rates and wages will remain sensitive to factors which are nothing to do with the university courses, but which reflect changes in the workplace and globalisation.

Measuring teaching excellence is an elusive but important challenge for HE and it is undoubtedly crucial that ideas about what excellent teaching is continue to be debated across the sector. However, as HERB begins to change the HE landscape there remain many unanswered questions about how effectively TEF will actually contribute to and inform that debate.

REFERENCES

Aubyn, M. St, Pina, G., & Pais. (2008). *Study on the efficiency and effectiveness of public spending on tertiary education*. Economic Paper No. 390, European Commission Research.

Ball, S. J. (2008). *The education debate: Policy and politics in the twenty-first century*. Bristol: Policy Press.

Barnett, R. (2007). *A will to learn. Being a student in an age of uncertainty*. Berkshire: Open University Press.

Bathmaker, A. M., Ingram, N., Abrahams, J., Hoare, A., Waller, R., & Bradley, H. (2016). *Higher education, social class and social mobility: The degree generation*. London: Palgrave Macmillan.

Bell, A., & Brooks, C. (2016). *Is there a magic link between research activity, professional teaching qualifications and student satisfaction*? Retrieved from http://ssrn.com/abstract=2712412. Accessed on May 12.

BIS. (2011). *Students at the heart of the system*. Retrieved from http://bis.gov.uk/assets/biscore/higher-education/docs/h/11-944-higher-education-students-atheart-of-system.pdf. Accessed on May 12, 2017.

BIS. (2015). *Fulfilling our potential: Teaching excellence, social mobility and student choice*. HMSO.

BIS. (2016b). *White Paper: Higher education: Teaching excellence, social mobility and student choice*. Retrieved from https://www.gov.uk/government/consultations/higher-education-teaching-excellence-social-mobility-and-student-choice. Accessed on May 12, 2017.

Blackmore, P., Blackwell, R., & Edmondson, M. (2016). *Tackling wicked issues: Prestige and employment outcomes in the teaching excellence framework*. HEPI Occasional Paper 14. Retrieved from http://www.hepi.ac.uk/2016/09/08/tackling-wicked-issues-prestige-employment-outcomes-teaching-excellence-framework/. Accessed May 12, 2017.

Boliver, V. (2011). Expansion, differentiation and the persistence of social class inequalities in British HE. *The International Journal of HE Research*, *61*(3), 229–242.

Boring, A., Ottoboni, K., & Stark, P. (2016). *Student evaluations of teaching (mostly) do not measure teaching effectiveness*. ScienceOpen Research.

Bradeley, S., Kirby, E., & Madriaga, M. (2015). What students value as inspirational and transformative teaching.

Innovations in Education and Teaching International, *52*(3), 231–242.

Britton, J., Dearden, L., Shephard, N., & Vignoles, A. (2016). *How English domiciled graduate earnings vary with gender, institution attended, subject and socio-economic background*. Institute of Fiscal Studies Working Paper. Retrieved from https://www.ifs.org.uk/uploads/publications/wps/wp201606.pdf. Accessed on May 12, 2017.

Browne, J. (2010). *Securing a sustainable future for higher education: An Independent Review of Higher Education Funding & Student Finance*. Retrieved from http://www.independent.gov.uk/browne-report. Accessed on May 12, 2017.

Brusoni, M., Radu, D., Grifoll Sauri, J., Jackson, S., Kömürcügil, H., Malmedy, M., … Zobeleds, L. (2014). *Report on the concept of excellence in higher education*. European Association for Quality Assurance in Higher Education (ENQA). Retrieved from http://www.enqa.eu/indirme/papers-and-reports/occasional-papers/ENQA%20Excellence%20WG%20Report_The%20Concept%20of%20Excellence%20in%20Higher%20Education.pdf. Accessed on June 1, 2017.

Christie, H. (2007). Higher education and spatial (im) mobility: Non-traditional students and living at home. *Environment and Planning*, *39*, 2445–2463.

Collini, S. (2016). Who are the spongers now? Review of fulfilling our potential: Teaching excellence, social mobility and student choice. *London Review of Books [Online]*, *38*(2) 33–37. Retrieved from https://www.lrb.co.uk/v38/n02/stefan-collini/who-are-the-spongers-now. Accessed on May 12, 2017.

Deem, R., Hillyard, S., & Reed, M. (2007). *Higher education and the new managerialism: The changing management of UK universities*. Oxford: Oxford University Press.

Department for Education and Skills. (2003). *The future of higher education*. London: DfES Publications.

Gibbs, G. (2010). *Dimensions of quality*. York: Higher Education Academy.

Gibbs, G. (2012). *Implications of 'dimensions of quality' in a market environment*. HEA Research Series. York: Higher Education Academy.

Goldstein, H. (2004). Education for All: The globalization of learning targets. *Comparative Education*, *40*(1), 7–14.

Goldthorpe, J. (2016). Social class mobility in modern Britain: Changing structure, constant process. *Journal of the British Academy*, *4*, 89–111.

Greatbatch, D., & Holland, J. (2016). *Teaching quality in higher education*. London: Department for Business, Innovation and Skills.

Gunn, V., & Fisk, A. (2013). *Considering teaching excellence in higher education: 2007–2013: A literature review since the CHERI Report 2007*. York: Higher Education Academy.

Hansard. (2017). *The official report of all parliamentary debates*. Retrieved from hansard.parliament.uk. Accessed on 21 May, 2017.

Harfold, T. (2014). Big data: A big mistake? *Significance*, *11*, 14–19.

Harvey, L. (2005). Embedding and integrating employability. *New Directions for Institutional Research*, *128*, 13–28.

HEFCE. (2016). *Review of information about learning and teaching, and the student experience. Results and analysis of the 2016 pilot of the National Student Survey*. Retrieved from http://www.hefce.ac.uk/media/HEFCE,2014/Content/Pubs/2016/201627/HEFCE2016_27.pdf. Accessed on 1 June, 2017.

Hénard, F., & Roseveare, D. (2012). *Fostering quality teaching in higher education: policies and practices: An institutional management guide for higher education institutions*. Paris: OECD.

High Level Group on the Modernisation of Higher Education. (2013). *Report to the European Commission: Improving the quality of teaching and learning in Europe's higher education institutions*. Retrieved from http://ec.europa.eu/education/highereducation/doc/modernisation_en.pdf. Accessed on June 1, 2017.

Higher Education and Research Act. (2017). *Higher Education and Research Act 2017* London: HMSO Retrieved from http://services.parliament.uk/bills/2016-17/highereducationandresearch.html. Accessed on June 1, 2017.

Higher Education Bill. (2003). HMSO.

Holmwood, J., Hickey, T., Cohen, R., & Wallis, S. (2016). *In defence of public higher education: Knowledge for a successful society. A response to 'success as a knowledge economy', BIS (2016)*. London: Convention for Higher Education.

Jones, I. (2010). Senses of belonging and fitting in? Affinities and emergent identities. *Widening Participation and Lifelong Learning*, *12*(2), 23–35.

Jump, P. (2015). REF 2014 rerun: Who are the 'game players'? *Times Higher Education*, January 2105. Retrieved from https://www.timeshighereducation.com/features/ref-

2014-rerun-who-are-the-game-players/2017670.article. Accessed on June 1, 2017.

Kelty, R., & Bunten, A. (2017). *Risk-taking in Higher Education, the importance of negotiating intellectual challenge in the college classroom*. Lanham, Boulder: Rowman & Little field Publishers.

Leathwood, C. (2010). Browne's recommendations will stop widening participation in its tracks', in Adults Learning. *NIACE*, *22*(2), 20–28.

Little, B., Locke, W., Parker, J., & Richardson, J. (Eds). (2007). Excellence in teaching and learning: A review of the literature for the Higher Education Academy. Centre for Higher Education Research and Information, The Open University, UK.

MacNell, L., Driscoll, A., & Hunt, A. N. (2015). What's in a Name: Exposing gender bias in student ratings of teaching. *Innovations in Higher Education*, *40*(4), 291–303.

McCaig, C., & Taylor, C. A. (2015). The strange death of Number Controls in England: Paradoxical adventures in higher education market making. *Studies in Higher Education*. Published online December 7, 2015.

McGettigan, A. (2013). *The Great University Gamble*. London: Pluto Press.

Neves, J., & Hillman, N. (2016). The 2016 Student Academic Experience Survey. *HEPI/HEA*. Retrieved from http://www.hepi.ac.uk/wp-content/uploads/2016/06/Student-Academic-Experience-Survey-2016.pdf. Accessed on June 1, 2017.

O'Leary, J. (2013). *The Sunday Times good university guide*. Glasgow: HarperCollins Publishers.

OECD. (2015). *Education at a glance, interim report: Update of employment and educational attainment indicators*. Retrieved from https://www.oecd.org/edu/EAG-Interim-report.pdf. Accessed on May 17, 2017.

Parpala, A., Lindblom-Ylänne, S., & Rytkönen, H. (2011). Students' conceptions of good teaching in three different disciplines. *Assessment & Evaluation in Higher Education*, *36*(5), 549–563.

Pleschová, G., Simon, E., Quinlan, K., Murphy, J., Roxa, T., & Szabó, M. (2012). The professionalisation of academics as teachers in higher education. *Standing Committee for Social Sciences: European Science Foundation*. Retrieved from http://www.esf.org/fileadmin/Public_documents/Publications/professionalisation_academics.pdf. Accessed on June 1, 2017.

Pollard, E. H., Williams, M., Buzzeo, J., Marvell, R., Tassinari, A., Bertram, B., & Fletcher, L., (Institute for Employment Studies); Artess, J., Redman, J. and Charlie Ball, (Higher Education Careers Services Unit) (2015). *Understanding employers' graduate recruitment and selection practices*. BIS Research Paper No. 231. HMSO.

Reay, D., Davies, J., David, M., & Ball, S. (2001). Choices of degree or degrees of choice? Class, 'race' and the higher education choice process. *Sociology*, *35*(4), 855–874.

Royal Statistical Society. (2017). Response to BIS Technical consultation on the teaching excellence framework about the TEF. *Royal Statistical Society*, Retrieved from http://www.rss.org.uk/Images/PDF/influencing-change/2016/RSS-response-to-BIS-TechnicalConsultation-on-Teaching-Excellence-Framework-year-2.pdf. Accessed on June 1, 2017.

Scott, P. (Ed.). (2000). *Higher education reformed*. London: Falmer Press.

Skelton, A. (Ed.). (2007). *International perspectives on teaching excellence in higher education: Improving knowledge and practice*. Abingdon: Routledge.

THE. (2016). Stern aims for lower REF workload, more 'game-changing' research *Times Higher Education*. Retrieved from https://www.timeshighereducation.com/news/stern-aims-lower-ref-workload-more-game-changing-research. Accessed on May 12, 2017.

Tinati, R., Halford, S., Carr, L., & Pope, C. (2014). Big data: Methodological challenges and approaches for sociological analysis. *Sociology*, *48*, 663–681.

UCU Workload Survey Report. (2016). Workload is an Education Issue'. *UCU Online* Retrieved from https://www.ucu.org.uk/media/8195/Workload-is-an-education-issue-UCU-workload-survey-report-2016/pdf/ucu_workloadsurvey_fullreport_jun16.pdf. Accessed on May 12.

UNESCO. (2002). *Education for All: An international strategy to put the Dakar framework for action on Education for All into operation*. Paris: UNESCO.

Vignoles, A. (2013). Social mobility, regression to the mean and the cognitive development of high ability children from disadvantaged homes. *Journal of the Royal Statistical Society. Series A: Statistics in Society*, 176, 887–906.

Which?. (2014). A degree of value: Value for money from the student perspective. *Which Online*, published November 2014. Retrieved from http://press.which.co.uk/wp-content/uploads/2014/11/Which-A-degree-of-value-Nov-2014.pdf. Accessed on May 12, 2017.

Wilsdon, J., Allen, L., Belfiore, E., Campbell, P., Curry, S., Hill, S., Jones, R., … Johnson, B. (2015). The metric tide: report of the Independent Review of the Role of Metrics. *Research Assessment and Management*. HEFCE.

Yorke, M. (2009). Student experience' surveys: Some methodological considerations and an empirical investigation. *Assessment & Evaluation in Higher Education*, *34*, 721–739.

3

FROM TEACHING EXCELLENCE TO EMERGENT PEDAGOGIES: A COMPLEX PROCESS ALTERNATIVE TO UNDERSTANDING THE ROLE OF TEACHING IN HIGHER EDUCATION

Phil Wood

INTRODUCTION

The relationship between teaching and universities has always been one of change and uneasiness. Historically, the role of universities centred on scholarship and research, with teaching used to fund the lives of university scholars. However, during the 19th century, the Humboldtian approach to higher education (HE), founded by the University of Berlin in 1810, became the accepted model for European universities. Research and teaching were seen as interconnected elements of university life, with both academics and students working together to pursue intellectual exploration. 'This ideal came to define the teacher–student relationship, which for Humboldt was one of the mutual dependence' (O'Byrne & Bond, 2014, p. 573). For a long period, extending into the 20th century, teaching was seen as central to the academic character of universities; as late as the 1960s some of the new universities in the UK were as well known for their experiments in teaching approaches as they were for their research (Anderson, 2010).

In contrast, with the introduction of the Research Assessment Exercise (RAE) in the late 20th century, together with research grant capture becoming a gauge of career success, research had become the dominant partner in many UK universities. Promotion to the higher ranks of academia was preferentially open to those with a long list of research publications and a 'track-record' of successful funded research projects. To reach an equal status through prolonged success and critical engagement with teaching was much more difficult. However, the emphasis has once again started to shift within the sector.

The publication of *Scholarship Reconsidered* by Boyer (1990) led to the emergence of the field of Scholarship of Teaching and Learning (SoTL). Boyer's work, alongside similar, contemporaneous developments such as the development of reflective practice (Schon, 1983, 1987) and Shulman's (1989) pedagogy of substance, led to a growing interest in developing critical understanding of HE teaching and the development of new practices. At the same time, the development of new frameworks for recognising quality in teaching, together with measures of student satisfaction of their university 'experience' also began to encourage, or force, universities to take the process of teaching seriously. This was further encouraged through the establishment of Centres of

Excellence in Teaching and Learning (CETLs) funded by the Higher Education Funding Council for England (HEFCE). As stated by Gosling and Hannan (2007, p. 634), this initiative was 'a major initiative designed both to reward and promote excellence in teaching and learning across the higher education curriculum'. At roughly the same time as this initiative developed, HEFCE also introduced the first National Teaching Fellowship awards, which eventually became the responsibility of the Higher Education Academy (HEA), created in 2003.

As discussed in Chapter 2 it is in an environment of increased marketisation within the sector that the new 'Teaching Excellence Framework' (TEF) has been established. However, what does 'teaching excellence' actually mean? If the TEF is truly an attempt to develop the quality of teaching in HE, what approaches to teaching and teaching development would help create better quality educational experiences for both students and academics? In considering these questions, this chapter outlines how teaching excellence has been understood in the past and why it might be a problematic concept. It then outlines one possible alternative way of understanding the nature and development of teaching based on a more emergent and collaborative view than that inherent in the current notion of teaching excellence.

WHAT IS TEACHING EXCELLENCE?

Teaching excellence is a difficult concept to define. The simplest way of attempting to characterise the phrase is to consider the definitions of the two words from which it is composed.

> *Teaching is the work that a teacher does in helping students to learn. (Collins online dictionary)*

> *[Excellence is] an action, characteristic, feature, etc, in which a person excels. (Collins online dictionary)*

From these definitions, teaching excellence is the work an individual excels at in aiding student learning. But such an explanation is a tautology, and has little explanatory power.

There is no shortage of research literature discussing the meaning of teaching excellence, but its heterogeneous nature is a common theme (e.g. see Piascik et al., 2011). Skelton (2004) stresses the contested and contingent nature of the term. He highlights the complex nature of an idea which shifts in meaning from context to context and over time. As a result, the best we can hope to achieve in trying to characterise teaching excellence is a general set of principles that together offer a basic framework. It is not possible to create a single, widely agreed definition.

Kreber (2002) argues that teaching excellence should be focused on 'performance' as it concerns the practice of teachers. This focus is differentiated from allied aspects of the teaching process such as scholarship of teaching which is research orientated and develops understandings of the nature of teaching. Consequently, Kreber begins to characterise teaching excellence as a process which can be based on the practical experience of the teacher, with little recourse to research; it is primarily about practice in the lecture hall or seminar room. She states that:

> *Excellence in teaching is usually identified on the basis of a judgement made about performance. Students, peers, and in some cases faculty members themselves describe how they perceive the performance (Kreber, 2002, p. 9).*

Teaching does not exist in a vacuum away from the needs and priorities of the wider academy, and as such, the nature of excellence is a reflection of wider institutional and sector-level pressures and contexts. As such, the nature of teaching excellence is both contested and contingent. It is not a constant. In turn, this shows that the very principle of 'excellence' is relative and may be in danger of becoming self-referential.

Skelton (2004) stresses that at the turn of the millennium, teaching excellence was underpinned by a commitment to reflective practice (Schön, 1983, 1987) whereby teachers identify issues through a continuous process of reflection in order to find ways to improve their performance. This is a similar argument to Kreber (2002), this process of reflection is practical in nature, relying on critical assessment and development of one's own practice. The recourse to research to embellish the lessons from reflection can occur, but is not central to the process.

Skelton's work highlighted a belief that teaching excellence included an ethical requirement to share and disseminate practice. This shows a moral imperative to share new practice and to play a role in helping others to develop their teaching. This then suggests that teaching excellence needs to be in some way a public process, a mechanism to tackle pedagogic solitude (Shulman, 1993), a situation where teachers act as isolated individuals as opposed to collaborative professionals.

The analysis of National Teaching Fellows' (NTF) reflections led Skelton (2004) to identify seven aspects of 'teaching excellence':

(1) reflecting on and meeting individual student needs

(2) starting from the place of students and promoting active learning

(3) communicating — knowing and valuing students through dialogue

(4) making use of technologies

(5) adopting problem-solving methodologies

(6) including the development of transferable skills

(7) offering learners flexibility and choice

This research begins to identify a wide-ranging concept which includes diverse approaches to teaching (such as problem-solving), personal and professional competences (such as reflective practice), and an ethical element emphasising a public imperative relating to sharing and advocating.

Skelton's (2004) multifaceted characterisation of teaching excellence is extended by Su and Wood (2012), who distinguish between two fundamentally different views of the role of the teacher. One perspective is a 'technical-rational' view which emphasises the skills, techniques and competences required for excellent practice, putting activity at the centre of the process. The alternative is a 'virtuous practice' view which instead emphasises the motivations, emotions and relationships involved. These two alternatives are similar in nature to those of Tubbs' (2005) philosophy of the teacher which differentiates between the 'teacher as master' and the 'teacher as servant'. The 'teacher as master' leads the imparting of knowledge in a subject-orientated classroom, whilst the teacher as servant's role is primarily to facilitate the interests and learning of students by supporting their discovery processes. These classifications emphasise that even the fundamental roles and identities of teachers are debateable as they tend towards very different views of the aims and processes at the core of successful teaching.

Like Skelton (2004), Shephard, Harland, Stein, and Tidswell (2010) base their insights concerning teaching excellence into the views of NTF awardees. The insights gained again, similar to Skelton, appear to be generally 'technical-rational' in nature, including:

(1) an emphasis on innovation,

(2) the development of authentic learning opportunities,

(3) the creation of meaningful learning activities,

(4) teacher-honesty,

(5) a match between teaching approaches and the situation,

(6) critical thinking approaches,

(7) student retention,

(8) high-quality feedback,

(9) inclusivity and pedagogic research

In contrast, Su and Wood (2012, p. 143) begin to develop the affective and moral aspects of teaching excellence, making a case for the essential inclusion of virtuous practice. They build on the work of Ayers (cited in Su & Wood, 2012, p. 143), who argued that teaching becomes 'mechanical and sterile, and learning the stuff of pigeons pecking for food' if it is not based on a vision, commitment, risk-taking and invention instead, energy, excitement and enthusiasm all become central. In addition, the relationships that emerge through the process of learning, understanding the needs of students, and basing practice on an ethical vision and commitment become central to what it means to foster teaching excellence.

Figure 3.1 offers some of the main dimensions that emerge from the literature. An important aspect of excellence is the practice of well-developed skills. These include aspects of

Figure 3.1. Simple Schematic of Overarching Elements of Teaching Excellence.

teaching, a variety of pedagogic approaches, such as the use and integration of technology, critical thinking and problem solving. To aid the continued development of practice, the need for reflection, and to a lesser extent research, is stressed. This can span a variety of activities from relatively informal personal reflections on teaching to more formal approaches to research in tandem with a spectrum of varied communal engagement, again from the personal to a pedagogic community of innovation. This then points to the importance of relationships, both between academics in developing teaching approaches and with students to create partnerships in advancing learning and teaching. Finally, these processes only work well if they are underpinned by enthusiasm and motivation for the tasks involved, driving academics' desire to develop better approaches and motivating students in their studies. At this more virtuous practice end of the scale, an ethical and affective imperative underlies the drive to expand and deepen the quality of pedagogic practice. Teaching excellence, therefore, inhabits a diverse and changing character. But as a result, can it really be treated as a meaningful and stable concept? If it is essentially fluid in nature can it be used as a general focus for pedagogic development? As discussed below, there are a number of arguments against the very use of the idea of 'excellence' in teaching.

THE PROBLEM WITH TEACHING EXCELLENCE

Whilst excellence might be a problematic concept, 'commitments to excellence occupy a largely unquestioned space in postsecondary education.' (Saunders, 2015, p. 393). But this important and generally accepted commitment towards excellence is increasingly being challenged through a number of objections.

Moore, Neylon, Eve, O'Donnell, and Pattinson (2016), focusing on narratives relating to research activity, critique the very term 'excellence'. They, like Saunders (2015), suggest that the term has come to permeate the sector, not only in establishing a yardstick against which to measure activity and performance, but also as a mainstay of advertising and strategic plans; if excellence is not claimed then a project or programme must be falling short in some way. As a consequence, 'excellence' might have become nothing more than an expected descriptor for things which are 'good', 'Centres of Excellence', 'Programmes of Excellence', or 'Global Excellence' may all begin to appear as no more than a form of advertising and/or virtue signalling. In this way the term becomes everything and nothing at the same time. As a result, Moore et al. (2016, p. 3) make the point that:

> *Because it lacks content, "excellence" serves in the broadest sense solely as an (aspirational) claim of comparative success: that some thing, person, activity, or institution can be asserted in a hopefully convincing fashion to be better or "more important" than some other...*

This quote demonstrates the weakness of excellence as a basis for describing teaching activities which are complex in nature, differing between disciplines, levels and contexts. It also implies the distorted importance of the issue in the current HE environment, where excellence becomes a competitive tool rather than a collaborative signifier. As discussed in Chapter 2, HE has become increasingly market-based, individuals have migrated from being 'students' to 'customers'. In this context the need to assure market position becomes important, and excellence becomes a natural, and explicit goal of the work of academics as it adds to the 'competitive edge' of the university. But excellence then becomes distorted in these narratives. Firstly, it is reconstituted, morphing from long-term application and personal development, to individual success measured against set criteria. This represents excellence as measurement, the criteria for which are decided by polices such as TEF to decide the rules of the game (Stilgoe, 2014). Excellence, therefore in the context of TEF, is not a framework to aid growth and discussion, but a measurement of public legitimacy.

Saunders (2015) argues that any use of excellence as a measure of standards begins to disintegrate under scrutiny because it is non-referential as it is not something which can be measured on its own terms. This leads Readings (1996, p. 22) to state that 'excellence has the singular advantage of being entirely meaningless'. He goes on to state, 'An excellent boat is not excellent by the same criteria as an excellent plane' (p. 24). Consequently, an excellent boat is only excellent in the context in which it will be used, and likewise for a plane. Transposed into an HE context, can we say that excellent teaching in one discipline can be easily or meaningfully transferred into, or measured against, another? Or that what is true of excellence in one department of economics holds exactly for another? So whilst excellence is widely used as if it has a common meaning across activities and contexts, this ubiquity actually undermines any meaningful use of the term. As such, the increasing measurement paradigm of excellence is fatally flawed.

Efficiency and accountability narratives are critiqued by Charles (2017), who stresses a developing link between teaching excellence and human capital theory. Much of the literature outlining the TEF is focused on competition, employability and productivity. These factors then stress a fundamental need for accountability and transparency and define an approach to teaching and learning which focuses on the development of 'transferable skills', 'employability' and 'digital literacy'. In turn, these skills sets are increasingly important in narratives referring to teaching excellence. As Charles remarks (2017, p. 8):

> *The focus on quality of education and on teaching excellence are connected to the need for state-directed interventions within the education industry in order to increase national productivity in the interests of capital.*

As a consequence of marketisation and accountability structures in HE, the sector has become increasingly anxious about the experience of students. HEIs are keen to demonstrate that student needs and wants are being met. However, such shifts, whilst making use of excellence as a unique selling point, could actually be responsible for a loss in academic professionalism and quality.

Biesta (2017, p. 320) stresses that the shift from student to customer has not led to the equal relationship advocated by those wanting democratisation in education. Instead, the relationship has increasingly become asymmetrical with academics expected to give student customers what they want.

But this mistakes the nature of the transaction between academic and student:

> *In economic transactions, customers know what they want and would just look for a company that can provide them ... a key aspect of professional relationships is that professional not just service the needs of their 'clients' [sic.] but also play a key role in the definition of what it is that their clients need.*

As the work of the teacher shifts towards an economic role, with the need for efficiency and positive outcomes, measurement and accountability agendas become ever more central to their work. The teacher needs to perform 'well', potentially putting a distorted notion of performance at the centre of the meaning of excellence. But such indicators see excellence as a reductive outcome rather than as the emergent, formative process as outlined by Kreber (2002). And it is here that a central concern of what teaching excellence is becoming can be found, that a narrative publicly claimed to focus on the development of teaching and learning is actually focused on ease of measurement (O'Neill, 2002) and increasing control of the teaching process in universities.

Teaching excellence now resides in a fundamentally ambiguous position in HE. For some it is a useful and formative concept, characterising the mixture of approaches, competences and dispositions which come together to offer a high-quality framework for developing teaching. But since the start of the new millennium, this formative narrative has been enveloped by three subsequent developments. The first was the 'codification' of excellence into lists which need to be met to allow an applicant to be publicly identified as 'excellent'. Examples of this shift include the HEA Fellowships system and university teaching excellence awards which demand academics show their expertise against a set of competences; these narratives increasingly need to be supported by examples of quantitative data, to prove that academics have reached a required outcome level. The second narrative is one which has emerged at the organisational level, an excellence aligned with the marketing and advertising imperative, excellence as a unique selling point to gain competitive advantage in the HE market place. The third is the most recent realisation of excellence, i.e. the focus on measurement and control, an excellence which in time may restrict and stifle democratic values, emphasising instead efficiency, human capital and the subordination of the professional autonomy of the academic teacher. But if the meaning of teaching excellence has been twisted and perverted over time, what might be developed in its place to help convey a process which centres on developing high-quality teaching in HE? The reversal of one aspect of teaching excellence, the reductive slide towards lists and outcome data, may be a good place to start. The antithesis of this position is a perspective that asks us to reconnect with the complexities of teaching and associated processes.

SKETCHING THE LANDSCAPE OF EMERGENT PEDAGOGIES

Teaching excellence may have started as a formative, process-driven idea. In fact, it is still the case that vestiges of this philosophy remain, as outlined in the loose framework summarising the literature earlier in this chapter (Figure. 3.1). However, this original orientation has been successively altered through various formal developments and the impact of marketization. What we now have is a teaching excellence which increasingly takes the form of a 'reductive materialism'. By this I mean that the richness, the contingent and contextual have been progressively eroded away. The complexity of practice has been captured and is being reduced by the creation of frameworks and evaluation rosters. Reduction is a natural and essential process. Biesta (2010b) points out that any complex system requires a level of reduction to make it understandable. The frameworks used in TEFs can be argued to offer a common language, a framework that is positive in promoting teaching as an important activity in the academy. However, the reductive nature of excellence frameworks has been transformed into hyper-reductionism through the creation of the TEF, as the complexity of teaching is increasingly boiled down to a few quantitative proxy indicators as discussed in Chapter 2.

As well as a trajectory towards reductionism there has also been a turn towards a form of materialism. Materialism holds that the fundamental nature of reality is based on matter rather than process. Teaching excellence can be argued to have moved towards this ontology. In TEF excellence is measured by outcomes, data and benchmarking. Teaching excellence, at this level, becomes something to be captured and owned as a thing. In relation to the TEF, that material ownership is even differentiated into a set of precious metals!

In choosing a reductive materialism, teaching itself is recast. It becomes focused on attaining particular, simple outcomes realised in the easiest, most cost-efficient ways possible. But this, one can argue, leads to a decline in the contextual, the contingent and the complex. Indeed, it may eventually lead towards the rise of 'corporate approaches' to teaching. In contrast, I argue that we need to move back towards an understanding of teaching as a complex process-led activity. As such, I argue that it is through engaging with aspects of complexity theory and process philosophy that we can reclaim a framework for teaching which centres on the multifaceted, the particular, and the continual emergence of new and coherent practices, what I call the development of 'emergent pedagogies'.

CAN WE TALK ABOUT TEACHING (ALONE)?

At a fundamental level can the idea of *teaching excellence* make sense? Characterising teaching as performance can give the impression that it is event-based, focused on an 'act' in a seminar room or lecture theatre. This leads to seeing teaching as an activity in its own right. But teaching only makes sense when we see it as intimately linked to the development of a curriculum which gives that teaching structure and coherence over time. And teaching and the curriculum on which it is based only make sense if we relate these processes to what we hope students will learn through engaging with them. Therefore, teaching cannot exist by itself as it only exists in relation to what is learned within the framework of a coherent curriculum. Finally, in formal HE at least, the degree to which students have learned anything needs to be gauged, leading to the need for assessment. As a result, we need to see teaching as a process which interpenetrates (Byrne & Callaghan, 2014) with the associated processes of curriculum, learning and assessment. To try to single out any one of these processes and treat it in isolation makes little sense.

How we characterise the nature of teaching matters, as our conceptualisation impacts on the way we understand and practice teaching, the same being true of our interaction with learning, curriculum and assessment. Because of the large number of elements at play, we can begin to understand teaching as a non-linear system. Teaching can be defined as a system as it is constituted of multiple features, factors and processes that interact at any instance in time. Non-linear systems are those in which these multiple elements create cause and effect relationships which are predominantly disproportionate in nature, and which interact in ever-shifting patterns. As a result, small causes may have very large impacts and vice versa. Consider the number of students, the technology they use and the multitude of spaces inhabited together with tutors and resources across any part of a module. The interrelationships and permutations involved are multiple and constantly changing. If we attempt to observe a seminar session we see a large number of interactions which also extend spatially and temporally beyond the face-to-face 'event' as students continue to engage with learning in different ways and in different locations, both pre- and post-session.

As a consequence, the interactions which occur during the process of learning are not predictable and 'linear'. Discussion and learning will not follow a strictly predetermined form or path that we are able to predict in anything other than the most general terms. Rich interactional activities will occur both between participants and between them and the various resources, media and spaces they use. As a consequence, for any given individual, elements of teaching that are expected to have an explicit impact on learning may actually have little effect whilst conversely a brief informal chat may be crucial in opening up the understanding of a concept or area of knowledge for an individual. As such, not only teaching, but learning, curriculum and assessment all need to be seen as non-linear in nature, and each as systems in their own right.

If we accept teaching as a non-linear system, we also need to consider how this system relates to other systems and the environment in which it is embedded. Some systems are 'closed' with limited interaction with the environment beyond. Any move away from an equilibrium state tends to lead to damping effects to bring it back towards near equilibrium. In other words, closed systems tend to be driven by negative feedback loops, but as such these systems tend to decay over time as they are divorced from external energy sources. In contrast, 'open' systems, of which most human systems are examples, can be impacted by the same negative feedback loops as those in closed systems, but may also be impacted by positive feedback which can move the system further away from equilibrium. It is the introduction of energy from the surrounding environment which keeps open systems in a state of flux and disequilibrium, but it is this energy which also leads to activity, emergence and change. One specific type of open system is the 'adaptive' system, commonly referred to in complexity theory as a *Complex Adaptive System* (CAS). In human systems, such as seminar rooms, the constant exchange of information between the system and the wider environment is responsible for its continued energy and ability to learn, and this constant input also allows the system to change and adapt. These systems have a number of features, the most important of which are discussed by Cilliers (1998) who characterises them as:

1. a large number of elements with many interactions;
2. interactions that are non-linear, i.e. large-scale causes can have small-scale impacts and vice versa;
3. interactions that lead to feedback loops, both negative and positive;
4. an 'open' system, having interactions with elements in external environments beyond the immediate system;
5. elements that interact with their environment making the identification of boundaries difficult;
6. a system that is far from equilibrium and therefore needs a constant energy flow for it to operate;

7. the importance of history, past processes playing a role in forming the present, often unpredictably;
8. each element only acting on local information rather than information from the whole system.

Seeing teaching as a complex adaptive system is to accept that it is not random, but neither is it wholly predictable and linear. It is constituted of many elements which change over time, and which are impacted by the history of the system, i.e. the way it changes is based in part on prior activity. In addition, if we accept that teaching is a complex adaptive system, then so too are learning, curriculum and assessment, as they are likewise constituted of a large number of non-linear, interacting elements. This means that rather than talking only of 'teaching' as if it is the singular defining process occurring in a seminar room or lecture hall, we need instead to expand out our thinking to encompass the interpenetration of four complex adaptive systems (Figure. 3.2)

Figure 3.2. Teaching within a Wider Framework of Complex Adaptive Systems.

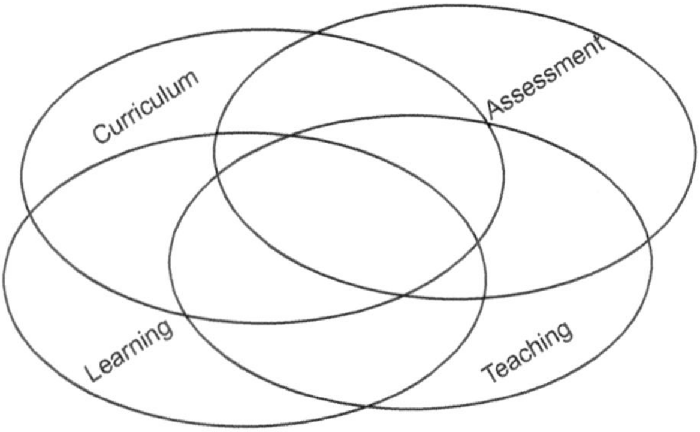

These four aspects together create the processes at the centre of interactions within and beyond the seminar room. But even here, we have an incomplete framework, as these systems are meaningless without the inclusion of the teacher and students (Figure. 3.3).

If we accept that these systems interpenetrate and act together through the collective actions of teachers and students, then to characterise the process as solely 'teaching' is no longer useful. As a consequence, teaching excellence is definably incoherent as a concept. How then might we refer to these complex processes? The terms we currently use are problematic in different ways, but heutagogy (Hase & Kenyon, 2000), andragogy (Knowles, 1970) or holiploigy (Wood, 2017) all at least move towards helping to capture the complexities of the processes involved. Here, for sake of

Figure 3.3. Teacher and Students at the Centre of a Complexity Orientated Process.

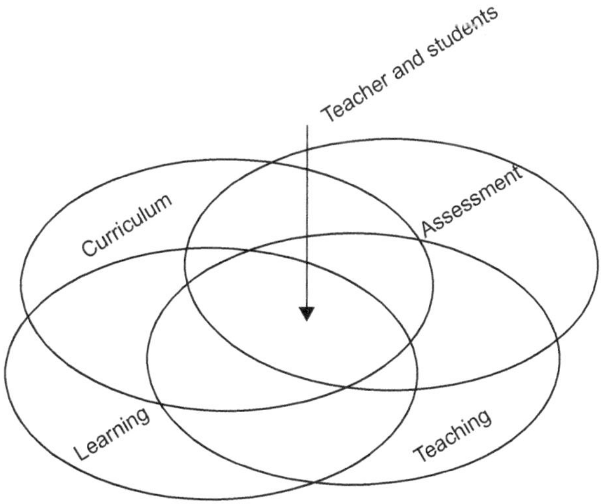

ease, I will use 'pedagogy'. Whilst accepting that it too retains 'cultural baggage' and connotations that may be less than helpful, not least the fact that it refers to the teaching of children, one advantage of using the term is that it can allow us to begin to capture the wider complexity of the processes involved.

As well as the struggle to find ways of conceptualising the system of processes involved in pedagogy, the acceptance of complexity creates a more fundamental challenge to the notion of 'excellence'. As discussed earlier in the chapter, excellence has increasingly become characterised by 'lists of good things', and/or thresholds in numeric data. To use these tools is to undertake the complexity reduction identified by Biesta (2010a). However, this is a dangerous process as the attempt to reduce the complexity of pedagogic processes potentially leads to the exclusion of large and important elements of its make-up. Conversely, Cilliers (1998, p. 13) argues that any total representation of a complex adaptive system would have to be as large as the system itself — a practical impossibility:

> *In building representations of open systems, we are forced to leave things out, and since the effects of these omissions are nonlinear, we cannot predict their magnitude.*

Consequently, Richardson, Cilliers, and Lissack (2007) refer to CASs as 'incompressible', and argue that to understand them, at last in part, we need to use different perspectives to build ever richer, if incomplete, models of the system we are interested in. To use a simple check list or framework to identify excellence is to undertake the folly of extreme complexity reduction until we are possibly no longer looking at the thing we wish to measure.

If we accept that pedagogy is constituted of interpenetrating complex adaptive systems, we also need to understand that interactions at any single point in time within a taught context are not of a random nature. The interactions, whilst complex, nevertheless have a level of coherence; they are not chaotic. In addition, the interactions involved also allow larger patterns to begin to form. Thus non-linear systems have the potential to create new properties from the interactions of the multitude of elements within them, properties which are not wholly predictable given the known starting-points within the system. For example, the drive through liminality towards the understanding of threshold concepts, central to the work of Meyer and Land (2003), can be characterised as the interplay of many elements which may lead to the emergence of new patterns of thinking and understanding which are not wholly recognisable from the constituent parts from which they spring. Consequently, emergence is the interplay of many properties over time and across scales which can lead to new states which are more than the sum total of the components themselves. In this way, the interplay of teaching, learning, curriculum and assessment leads to pedagogy as an emergent network of processes.

In considering how we might move forward from focusing solely on teaching, a complexity perspective leads us towards a more holistic notion of the processes involved, and recasts (not perfectly) this series of complex adaptive systems as a form of 'pedagogy'. However, even by characterising pedagogy in this way, we are excluding one further crucial component. Processes, which are woven throughout this model, occur over time. As Rescher (2000, p. 6) emphasises from a process philosophical perspective; temporality, activity, and change — of alteration, striving, passage, and novelty-emergence — are the cardinal factors for our understanding of the real.

In other words, time needs to be included in our characterisation of pedagogy. By including time, pedagogy, seen as the interaction of components, processes, and past practice is always open to new and unexpected configurations. In other words, as discussed above, pedagogy is emergent. Through careful attention to practice and context, we are able to experience and create emergent pedagogies, a combination of complexity and process over time to bring new, and sometimes unpredicted, practice to aid student learning. If this is the case, how can we create productive environments which encourage and engage individuals in developing such emergent pedagogies?

THE GROWTH OF EMERGENT PEDAGOGIES

In considering how we develop our practice as teachers, I will use some of the insights of Cajkler and Wood (2016), who outlined the characteristics of what they refer to as pedagogic literacy. One observation they make is that humans have the capacity to both learn and teach. Children teach each other games, parents teach their children how to tie their shoe laces, how to behave and how to ride a bicycle. Individuals teach others how to carry out tasks. Therefore, teaching is as ubiquitous as learning; it is part of the human experience.

If all humans have a capacity to teach, what makes teachers distinctive? Crucial processes involve teachers focusing their professional work on understanding and developing their practice whilst also developing their subject knowledge, leading to the shaping of pedagogic content knowledge (Shulman, 1986, 1987). By specialising in pedagogy, teachers move from an informal process of teaching, i.e. trial and error, often implicit and subconscious, to one which is made explicit, which is constantly problematised, and around which can be built structures and processes to enable better, more effective and more creative ways to help others learn. Therefore, what distinguishes teachers from others is a heightened awareness, understanding and pursuit of better pedagogy. Cajkler and Wood (2016) identify seven 'dimensions' that together lead to greater pedagogic literacy. Here, I simplify these to five foci which can help us to understand and explain the growth of emergent pedagogies in HE contexts (Table 3.1). This table must be seen as only indicative. As discussed earlier, complex systems are incompressible (Richardson et al., 2007). Any attempt to charcterise them must lead to a level of complexity reduction (Biesta, 2010b) and therefore any model must be, by its nature, incomplete. Here, what is offered is an indication, not a roadmap.

The complexity of pedagogy is such that we must continue to develop our understanding over the course of many years; in fact, from a complexity perspective it is a truism that we will never have either a perfect understanding of the processes of pedagogy or ever teach the perfect lesson over the course of our career's span. Pedagogic environments are complex adaptive systems in which teachers constantly move between, and simultaneously engage with each of the different foci in Table 3.1. As an example, if a student does not understand a concept or area of knowledge, the values of the individual (affective foundations) will work with their professional skills and understanding (personal growth) whilst also operating within the organisational and societal contexts to develop pedagogic solutions to aid understanding. The enactment of emergent pedagogies is the interplay between these different foci and the processes within them over time.

It is the wide range of knowledge, skills, values and contexts inherent in the pedagogic environment, which lead to

Table 3.1. An Outline of Indicative Foci Supporting Emergent Pedagogies.

Societal Contexts	• Policy • Socio-economic and cultural change
Organisational Contexts	• University and disciplinary cultures • Programme Regulations
Collaborative Growth	• Professional development • Collaborative development and learning • Research
Personal Growth	• Professional skills (explaining, seminar room management, assessment) • Understanding learning, pedagogic content knowledge • Experience and reflection • Research
Affective Foundations	• Values • Attitudes • Philosophies

Present practice ← *TIME/EMERGENCE* → *Future practice*

the growth of teachers' emergent practice. However, these emergent processes are not, by definition, deterministic and neither are they purely positive in nature; practice does not automatically follow a virtuous path towards ever greater insight and success.

Our values, attitudes and philosophies (hereafter referred to simply as values) are part of what makes us who we are.

They are the lens through which we perceive the world, impacting on our beliefs concerning issues such as politics and the environment. This makes values central to any activity we undertake as they guide our thinking and act as a framework which scaffolds the decisions we make and the reasons we find important in justifying our actions. This is no less true of the decisions we make as teachers regarding the pedagogies we believe we should foster in helping students reach their potential.

It takes a deep engagement with ideas and values to affect changes in the way individuals work as professionals. It is also in the dissonance between organisational expectation and personal values that stress and disillusionment can begin to occur, especially where authenticity of purpose and practice is dissonant between individual and organisation. The negotiation of values through teaching is considered by Skelton (2012), who identifies different levels at which we need to negotiate our values and understand them against the constraints we may experience:

> *Initial and continuing professional development... about teaching and learning represent[s] important spaces where people can explore and develop their educational values and learn from the examination of value conflicts. To be authentic, such spaces need to acknowledge the micro, meso and macro level constraints that may make it difficult to realise particular educational values and to support people in developing personal responses to such circumstances. (p. 267)*

Kreber (2010) argues that with increasing complexity in the relationships between research, teaching and administration together with greater accountability in HE, authenticity can indeed be lost. Consequently, Nixon, Marks, Rowland, and Walker (2001) argue that this has played a role in a shift from the good of education to education as a good. To understand the degree to which our pedagogic values can be realised, or undermined, we need to have an understanding of all five foci of emergent pedagogies. We need to understand and develop our personal attributes, we need to achieve this by acting collaboratively (at least some of the time), whilst understanding the potential impact of organisational and societal values and processes on our practice. In this way, values, attitudes and philosophies are at the core of emergent pedagogies.

The individual teacher can develop their professional skills over time, including core aspects of pedagogic practice such as lecturing, assessment or the development of module content. The development of knowledge and skills comes from a core of experience and reflection (Schön, 1983). Over time, it is possible for teachers to become ever more expert in delivering their ideas and interacting with students. One way of considering the interplay of factors which are important is that of pedagogic content knowledge (Shulman, 1986, 1987) which sees high-quality practice resulting from a deep understanding of the subject knowledge to be covered, enfolded with a critical and deep understanding of pedagogic approaches which help the teacher to use which ever approach they believe to be most appropriate in any given situation, resulting in a flexibility to call on other approaches if the one they have chosen appears not to work. Such flexibility only comes from long experience, reflection and understanding and a desire to know more about pedagogic practice, and the way in which people learn. Reading or carrying out research relating to pedagogy will also add to the experience, knowledge and practice for some individuals.

Whilst the development of Scholarship for Teaching (Boyer, 1990) started to open up the potential for more collaborative pedagogic work in HE, Shulman (1993) identified the presence of a 'pedagogic solitude', with many academics working alone and sharing little. He therefore called for the development of communities of researcher–teachers who are willing to discuss, share and publish their work on pedagogy, resulting in his idea of 'Teaching as Community Property'.

Collaboration has become an increasingly popular tenet of professional development and learning. It has an obvious attraction as it gives, as Shulman suggests, an opportunity for sharing, critiquing and developing pedagogic ideas and approaches; it is at the heart of SoTL. Hargreaves and Fullan (2012) contextualise collaboration explicitly within their theory of Professional Capital. The case they make is that if we are to enable the growth of critical, professional teachers they need the opportunity to develop their understanding and practice through three 'channels' together creating professional capital.

$$\text{Professional Capital} = \text{Human Capital} + \text{Social Capital} + \text{Decisional Capital}$$

Here, the growth of the individual's practice (Human Capital) through the development of valuable knowledge and skills is seen as best achieved through regular collaborative work (Social Capital) within a context where teachers can make authentic and meaningful judgements (Decisional Capital) to develop and innovate their shared practices. We all bring unique perspectives, knowledge and experiences to pedagogic development and we need to ensure, within collaborative contexts, that the agency of practitioners is retained, each taking what they value from the collaboration whilst not feeling pressured to agree to a 'group-approach'. In considering the development of emergent pedagogies, there is both personal and collaborative growth, but these occur in tension. We must accept that individuals will take different lessons and insights from working together. Hence, all individuals will to some extent develop unique pedagogic practice. Learning and development exists neither solely within the individual nor the group but within and between them.

At a higher level, the ways in which both individuals and groups act within an organisation are partly the consequence of organisational contexts. The development of a new programme, for example will need to abide by regulations set out by the organisation. How individuals navigate the potential tensions between their own values and practices and organisational regulations is part of the pedagogic role. Organisations will also have wider regulations relating to issues such as feedback, the roles of students in their learning, student voice and inclusion. All such organisational structures and policies will need to be understood and incorporated into the work of individuals. In fact, where some of these regulations clash with the value judgements of teachers, there may be tensions regarding the degree to which they can be ignored or subverted. These issues demonstrate that an important element of the emerging pedagogies which individuals foster relates to the organisational contexts teachers find themselves in, and hence how they learn to navigate the tensions between their professional pedagogic beliefs and practices, and those of the university. It becomes a process of understanding and negotiating how to increase the opportunity spaces to create the freedom to fulfil values and professional practice.

Finally, we need to understand the university sector, and the pedagogic work that occurs within it, as developing within wider societal contexts. The university sector, like any other, is exposed to regular national policy shifts. As a consequence, policy, such as that surrounding tuition fees or the loss of State subsidy for teaching, and most recently the introduction of the TEF play a major role in the way in which social and political change impacts on the university sector. Likewise, the continued move to concentrate research funding in the sciences and engineering, and a move towards more focused funding of quantitative research in the Social Sciences create major shifts in the ways universities see themselves and the activities they decide to promote. All of these policies play a part in altering the dynamics of university activity, including teaching. Therefore, to understand these contexts in building pedagogic models we need to have an understanding of the policy trajectories, the changing regulatory frameworks that surround them and the ways in which we can, where we feel it necessary, resist or subvert them.

There are also constant shifts beyond the university sector. New and different patterns are emerging at both societal and global level. Modern patterns of globalisation are constantly shifting. Capital transfers, changes in working practices and the rise of artificial intelligence, as well as the more rapid and mass movement of people are all being challenged and questioned. Alongside these shifting patterns have come a transformation in the role and character of universities over recent years, particularly since the opening up of former communist states. This reverberates through the university sector in a number of ways. First we had league tables for British universities — then in the last few years this has been added to by numerous global league tables. Why? Because league tables, like PISA in the school sector, are essential data for economic processes, in the case of HE for those making global choices about university applications, and for those deciding where their investments should flow. This has led to a huge financial inflow to the UK through large numbers of students from countries such as China. This in turn has important implications for pedagogy as even relatively small groups of international students may have an array of prior learning experiences, knowledge, expectations as to the meaning of 'study' and even rules concerning plagiarism or referencing. Hence, large-scale processes beyond the academy are having potentially major impacts on the work of teachers.

New pedagogies emerge through the interplay of processes over different spatial, temporal and conceptual scales. Values, personal growth, collaborative endeavour and an understanding of organisational and societal contexts are all important in the growth of new pedagogic practices. But perhaps most crucial is the need to understand that these processes interact in different ways, in different contexts and through the work of different individuals and groups. This is what makes the pedagogy emergent. It is also what makes any reference to an overarching definition of 'teaching excellence' impossible.

SOME FINAL REMARKS

The work of teachers in HEIs is complex, meaning that their practices are multidimensional in nature. I characterise this work as complex-process orientated, a counter to reductive definitions of teaching. A complex-process orientation also rejects the individualistic notions of teacher work which is inherent in 'excellence' awards. Such awards often ask teachers to identify the work which belongs to them, rather than emphasising the collegial and emergent nature of pedagogy. A complex-process approach also rejects increasingly simplistic quantitative proxies as exemplified by the TEF, metrics, league tables, simplistic quality assurance frameworks and over-generalised evaluation tools. As Halachmi (2014) states:

> *The paradox is that the accountability fervor meant to assure performance can have direct and indirect consequences that undermine it.*

To ensure that the quality of teaching develops within the HE system, we need to worry less about public identification of excellence, and instead focus our efforts on understanding and developing great practice. This emerges from collegial work, and therefore requires senior managers to micro-manage less. The focus needs to shift away from paperwork, which only functions to divert energy from practice, and instead empower and enable academics to develop their teaching as professionals.

A complex-process approach to pedagogy argues for the need to consider the interplay of teaching with curriculum, assessment and learning. It also stresses the constant flow and change in participants, processes and contexts and the links between them. If accepted as offering a useful view of the work of teachers, these perspectives have major ramifications for the way academics and universities understand pedagogy and the nature of their work. It suggests a turn towards collegiality and away from the 'hero' academic. At present applications for fellowships and promotions ask the individual to stress their personal role. Narratives become focused on the 'I', the 'me' rather than the 'we' or the 'us'. The latter is pathologised as a weakness. But our work is only ever part of a wider, emergent collegial whole, be that through work with other academics and/or students.

In putting forward the idea of emergent pedagogies as a basis for the growth of great teaching in HE, there is a return to something like a Humboldtian philosophy. It is based on academics and students working together to create and develop academic experiences which are worthwhile and transformative to both. It is a philosophy that deliberately turns away from a reductive, utilitarian view of teaching, and instead replaces it with a community-driven, contextually rich mix of processes fundamental to the emergence of high-quality learning and both personal and communal growth.

REFERENCES

Anderson, R. (2010). *The 'Idea of a University' today.* History and Policy, Policy Paper. Retrieved from http://www.historyandpolicy.org/policy-papers/papers/the-idea-of-a-university-today

Biesta, G. (2010a). *Good education in an age of measurement: Ethics, politics, democracy.* Boulder, CO: Paradigm Publishers.

Biesta, G. (2010b). Five theses on complexity reduction and its politics. In D. Osberg & G. Biesta (Eds.), *Complexity theory and the politics of education* (pp. 5–14). Amsterdam: Sense Publishers.

Biesta. (2017). Education, measurement and the professions: Reclaiming a space for democratic professionality in education. *Educational Philosophy and Theory*, *49*(4), 315–330. doi:10.1080/00131857.2015.1048665

Boyer, E. L. (1990). *Scholarship reconsidered: Priorities of the professoriate.* Princeton, NJ: Carnegie Foundation for the Advancement of Teaching.

Byrne, D., & Callaghan, G. (2014). *Complexity theory and the social sciences: The state of the art.* Abingdon: Routledge.

Cajkler, W., & Wood, P. (2016). Lesson study and pedagogic literacy in initial teacher education: Challenging reductive models. *British Journal of Educational Studies*, *64*(4), 503–521. Retrieved from http://www.tandfonline.com/doi/abs/10.1080/00071005.2016.1164295

Charles, M. (2017). Teaching, in spite of Excellence: Recovering a Practice of Teaching-Led Research. *Studies in Philosophy and Education*, First Online. doi:10.1007/s11217-017-9568-1

Cilliers, P. (1998). *Complexity and postmodernism: Understanding complex systems*. London: Routledge.

Gosling, D., & Hannan, A. (2007). Responses to a policy initiative: The case of Centres for Excellence in Teaching and Learning. *Studies in Higher Education*, *32*(5), 633–646.

Halachmi, A. (2014). Accountability overloads. In M. Bovens, R. E. Goodin, & T. Schillemans (Eds.), *The Oxford handbook of public accountability*. Oxford: Oxford University Press.

Hargreaves, A., & Fullan, M. (2012). *Professional capital: Transforming teaching in every school*. New York, NY: Teachers' College Press.

Hase, S., & Kenyon, C. (2000). *From andragogy to heutagogy*. Ultibase, RMIT [Online]. Retrieved from http://pandora.nla.gov.au/nph-wb/20010220130000/http://ultibase.rmit.edu.au/Articles/dec00/hase2.htm. Accessed on April 3, 2017.

Knowles, M. S. (1970). *The modern practice of adult education. Andragogy versus pedagogy*. Englewood Cliffs, NJ: Prentice Hall/Cambridge.

Kreber, C. (2002). Teaching excellence, teaching expertise, and the scholarship of teaching. *Innovative Higher Education*, *27*, 5–23.

Kreber, C. (2010). Academics' teacher identities, authenticity and pedagogy. *Studies in Higher Education, 35*(2), 171–194. doi:10.1080/03075070902953048

Meyer, J. H. F., & Land, R. (2003). *Threshold concepts and troublesome knowledge: Linkages to ways of thinking and practising within the disciplines enhancing teaching-learning environments in undergraduate courses.* Occasional Report 4, May 2003. Retrieved from http://www.etl.tla.ed.ac.uk/docs/ETLreport4.pdf. Accessed on May 29, 2017.

Moore, S., Neylon, C., Eve, M. P., O'Donnell, D. P., & Pattinson, D. (2016). "Excellence R Us": University research and the fetishisation of excellence. *Palgrave Communications*. doi:10.1057/palcomms.2016.105. Retrieved from http://www.palgrave-journals.com/articles/palcomms2016105

Nixon, J., Marks, A., Rowland, S., & Walker, M. (2001). Towards a new academic professionalism: A manifesto of hope. *British Journal of Sociology of Education*, 22(2), 227–244.

O'Byrne, D., & Bond, C. (2014). Back to the future: The idea of a university revisited. *Journal of Higher Education Policy and Management*, 36(6), 571–584, doi:10.1080/1360080X.2014.957888

O'Neill, O. (2002). *BBC Reith lectures 2002. A question of trust*. Retrieved from http://www.bbc.co.uk/radio4/reith2002

Piascik, P., Bouldin, A., Schwarz, L., Pittenger, A., Medina, M., Rose, R., & Hammer, D. (2011). Rewarding teaching excellence in pharmacy teaching. *Currents in Pharmacy Teaching and Learning*, 3, 249–254.

Readings, B. (1996). *The university in ruins*. Cambridge, MA: Harvard University Press.

Rescher, N. (2000). *Process philosophy: a survey of basic issues.* Pittsburgh, PA: University of Pittsburgh Press.

Richardson, K. A., Cilliers, P., & Lissack, M. (2007). In P. Cilliers (Ed.), *Complexity science: A 'Gray' science for the 'Stuff in Between' in thinking complexity: Complexity and philosophy* (Vol. 1, pp. 25–35). Mansfield, MA: ISCE Publishing.

Saunders, D. B. (2015). Resisting excellence: Challenging neoliberal ideology in postsecondary education. *Journal for Critical Education Policy Studies, 13*(2), 391–413.

Schön, D. (1983). *The reflective practitioner, how professionals think in action.* New York, NY: Basic Books.

Schon, D. A. (1987). *Educating the reflective practitioner: Toward a new design for teaching and learning in the professions.* San Francisco, CA: Jossey-Bass.

Shephard, K., Harland, T., Stein, S., & Tidswell, T. (2010). Preparing an application for a higher-education teaching-excellence award: Whose foot fits Cinderella's shoe? *Journal of Higher Education Policy and Management, 33*(1), 47–56.

Shulman, L. S. (1986). Those who understand: Knowledge growth in teaching. *Educational Researcher, 15*, 4–14.

Shulman, L. S. (1987). Knowledge and teaching: Foundations of the new reform. *Harvard Educational Review, 57*, 1–22.

Shulman, L. S. (1989). Toward a pedagogy of substance. *AAHE Bulletin, 41*(10), 8–13.

Shulman, L. S. (1993). Teaching as community property: Putting an end to pedagogical solitude. *Change, 25*(6), 6–7.

Skelton, A. (2004). Understanding ‘teaching excellence’ in higher education: A critical evaluation of the National Teaching Fellowship Scheme. *Studies in Higher Education, 29*(4), 451–468.

Skelton, A. (2012). Value conflicts in higher education teaching. *Teaching in Higher Education, 17*(3), 257–268.

Stilgoe, J. (2014). Against Excellence. *The Guardian,* December 19. Retrieved from https://www.theguardian.com/science/political-science/2014/dec/19/against-excellence

Su, F., & Wood, M. (2012). What makes a good university lecturer? Students’ perceptions of teaching excellence. *Journal of Applied Research in Higher Education, 4*(2), 142–155.

Tubbs, N. (2005). *Philosophy of the teacher*. Oxford: Blackwell.

Wood, P. (2017). Holiploigy – Navigating the complexity of teaching in higher education. *Journal of Learning Development in Higher Education*, 11, 1–9 [online]. Retrieved from http://www.aldinhe.ac.uk/ojs/index.php?journal=jldhe&page=article&op=view&path%5B%5D=421

4

MONITORING AND MEASURING TEACHING EXCELLENCE IN HIGHER EDUCATION: FROM CONTRIVED COMPETITION TO COLLECTIVE COLLABORATION

Matt O'Leary

INTRODUCTION

In 2016 the British government introduced the Teaching Excellence Framework (TEF). In the lead up to the TEF, the quality of teaching in Higher Education Institutions (HEIs) had come in for criticism by some in government circles, notably David Willetts the Minister of State for Universities and Science from 2010 to 2014, who claimed that teaching was 'by far the weakest aspect of English higher education' and was an area in urgent need of monitoring and improvement (Gill, 2015). Both Willetts and his incumbent Jo

Johnson asserted the need for HE teaching to adopt a more evidence-based approach to practice akin to that associated with research. Yet, ironically, neither drew on any such evidence to support their critiques, relying instead on unsubstantiated assumptions and anecdotes.

As further justification for the introduction of the TEF, the government argued that it would help to identify, encourage and reward excellence in teaching and as such become a key lever in driving up standards across HEIs (BIS, 2016). A key premise underpinning the government's argument was that if teaching were to be considered of equal value to research, then an equivalent scheme to the Research Excellence Framework would need to be established to enable the monitoring and measurement of the quality of teaching across individual HEIs. In keeping with its adherence to neoliberal policy making, the government thus decided that for the TEF to achieve its desired outcomes, it was important to create the conditions for free market competition amongst providers, which would, in the government's eyes, naturally result in each HEI striving for excellence in teaching.

It is fair to say that the reaction to the TEF of those working in the sector has been mixed to date. Whilst some welcome it as overdue acknowledgement of the importance of teaching and its perceived undervaluing compared to research in universities, others are more sceptical of the rationale for its creation and its underlying purpose(s). On the one hand, some see the TEF as an opportunity for a greater focus and investment in teaching. On the other hand, there are those who regard it as yet another example of the marketisation of HE and a continuing neoliberal agenda to impose free market principles and practices on the sector. The reliance on the use of a core set of metrics (see below for further discussion) that have contested and tenuous links to teaching quality has been the target of criticism of many commentators, not to mention the adoption of a one-size-fits-all framework that seems ill-equipped to consider HEIs' differing contexts and cultures. In discussing the current obsession with national and international league tables and the wider role of universities, Collini (2012) is critical of the rationale for the creation of schemes like the TEF, along with the overreliance on reductive statistical data valued by so many senior leaders and policy makers:

> *The second force is the growing distrust of reasoned argument, now often seen as a cloak for special interests or a form of elitist arrogance, and the substitution in its place of any kind of indicator that can plausibly be reduced to numerical terms. The latter possess the aura of both precision and objectivity and so, when joined with the assumption about competition, can generate a definitive ranking. (p. 17)*

Collini raises important questions about the role and impact of marketised competition in the work of universities and how they are judged and valued by others in society. Added to this is the nature of the evidence relied upon to assess the quality and/or effectiveness of their work, what it actually reveals about the work in question and its impact on institutions and individuals alike. These are issues that will be explored throughout this chapter.

DEFINING TEACHING EXCELLENCE

Is it possible to talk about teaching excellence in HE in a generic sense? Excellent for whom, for what purpose and when? Excellence is a ubiquitous term that permeates the discourse of education policy and practice. There is no shortage of speeches and publications in which politicians and policy makers proclaim the importance of creating, capturing and championing excellence in education, but rarely is the term interrogated or defined. As Collini (2012, p. 109) argues, there is a 'vacuity' associated with the term when used in the context of policy debates about raising standards and improving quality:

> *... there is no such thing as excellence in the abstract, and it only makes sense as a descriptive term when there is a) agreement about the character and worth of the relevant activity in the first place, and b) some agreed means of arriving at comparative judgements of how far any one instance embodies more of that worth.*

Despite the differing perspectives and focus of each of the chapters in this book, the difficulty of defining excellence in teaching is something that is acknowledged by each author. Yet given the diversity and complexity of the sector, it should come as no surprise to anyone involved in HE that agreeing on a standardised definition of teaching excellence should be so problematic. It is precisely because teaching is a complex, multi-faceted and contextually dependent process that reaching a consensus on a common definition in a specified context is an incredibly difficult task, let alone extending this to a country's education system or even more widely internationally. As stated in the previous chapter, the best we can then therefore hope to achieve is to establish a general set of principles that might act as a central reference point. But what might these principles look like? Here is where it can be useful to draw on relevant education research. And what could be more appropriate to start with than cognate work in the field by the chair of the TEF assessment panel, Professor Chris Husbands?

In a report entitled *What makes great pedagogy? Nine claims from research*, Husbands and Pearce (2012) examined the literature on teacher effectiveness and set out nine claims about what makes for great pedagogic practices drawing on a range of research evidence. They concluded that:

> *Highly successful pedagogies develop when teachers make outstanding use of their understanding of the research and knowledge-base for teaching in order to support high-quality planning and practice. The very best teaching arises when this research base is supplemented by a personal passion for what is to be taught and for the aspirations of learners. (p. 12)*

Husbands and Pearce's conceptualisation of 'highly successful pedagogies' accentuates the central role of research, reinforcing the notion of a symbiotic relationship between teaching and research. But to what extent is this borne out in practice? Is what teachers do underpinned by pedagogic research and if so, how is this manifested in their decision making at the stages of planning, delivery and assessment? In the schools' sector, the emergence of virtual (e.g. Twitter) and actual (e.g. TeachMeet) teacher communities in recent years with a focus and interest in pedagogy has certainly triggered a growth in teachers' exposure to and engagement with pedagogic research and knowledge exchange. This is ostensibly because what was once reserved for members of a small, restricted community (i.e. those with access to academic journals, conferences, etc.) has since been opened up to include audiences that are much more inclusive and representative of the teaching profession as a whole. However, the extent to which academic staff in HE actively make use of education research to inform and support their teaching practice is an area of inquiry itself that would benefit from further research as it is not yet fully understood.

The nine claims identified by Husbands and Pearce (2012) in their study were as follows:

1. Effective pedagogies give serious consideration to pupil voice.
2. Effective pedagogies depend on behaviour (what teachers do), knowledge and understanding (what teachers know) and beliefs (why teachers act as they do).
3. Effective pedagogies involve clear thinking about longer term learning outcomes as well as short-term goals.
4. Effective pedagogies build on pupils' prior learning and experience.
5. Effective pedagogies involve scaffolding pupil learning.
6. Effective pedagogies involve a range of techniques, including whole-class and structured group work, guided learning and individual activity.
7. Effective pedagogies focus on developing higher order thinking and metacognition, and make good use of dialogue and questioning in order to do so.
8. Effective pedagogies embed assessment for learning.
9. Effective pedagogies are inclusive and take the diverse needs of a range of learners, as well as matters of student equity, into account.

It is interesting to note the similarities between the nine claims listed above and the seven aspects of teaching excellence identified by Skelton (2004) in his work, as outlined by Phil Wood in the previous chapter. The similarities between these two taxonomies are made all the more interesting when we consider that Skelton's work centred on the teaching of adults in the HE environment, whereas Husbands and

Pearce's study focused on the teaching of children in the schools' sector. Thus despite these two very differing contexts, commonalities clearly exist, which would suggest a core set of principles of effective teaching that may even transcend contextual boundaries. For example, both taxonomies emphasise the importance of inclusivity and the centrality of considering students when it comes to making decisions about the curriculum, pedagogy and assessment. Equally, the importance of dialogue and communication is highlighted as a crucial element of teacher–student interaction, which itself needs to be underpinned by the teacher having a sound understanding of pedagogy and theories of learning. Furthermore, this common core of principles is echoed in the findings of the Teaching and Learning Research Programme, the largest and lengthiest study ever conducted into teaching and learning in the United Kingdom (see James & Pollard, 2011).

When asked to discuss *What is excellent teaching?* as part of a 2016 conference workshop, members of university teaching staff from a range of different disciplines and faculties commented that the key starting point for their group discussion was how excellence was often perceived as a challenging and contested term amongst academics. Especially for those working in or with a background in education, where it is a term that has become part of a colonised discourse associated with external agencies such as Ofsted; a marketised term that lacks clarity and shifts according to the role and purpose of its user. At the same time, it is one that projects a particular conceptualisation of the role of academic teaching staff and what is expected of them by those involved and with an interest in the teaching–learning interface.

An alternative term suggested by some education and health practitioners was that of teaching being 'fit for purpose'. In other words, the extent to which the teaching approach adopted by academic staff best meets the needs of their students and what they are required or expected to do with what they are taught.

The identities and backgrounds of students emerged as a key driver for making decisions about excellence in teaching as there was a consensus around the notion that 'excellent teachers' shape and adapt their teaching according to their students' needs, once again echoing some of the research findings. It was also acknowledged that external agents such as examiners and moderators have an important role to play in terms of stimulating discussion on the 'best practice' that they have identified in their capacity as independent assessors.

Table 4.1 captures an indicative sample of the participants' comments. Overall, it was interesting to note that many of the key discussion points to emerge from this interdisciplinary workshop on teaching excellence resonated with findings from recent cognate literature and research in HE (e.g. Greatbatch & Holland, 2016; Skelton, 2004). In particular, the importance of engaging with and responding to students' needs, as well as the changing nature of conceptualisations of excellence, contextually and temporally.

A further confounding variable in defining excellence in teaching that has received little attention in recent debates is identifying what actually constitutes teaching in the HE environment. Teaching in HE has moved a substantial way from the traditional lecturing mode that has been associated with the sector for so long. Yet as the following chapter in this book points out in drawing on the work of Gunn and Fisk (2013), there is a 'lack of sophistication in the conceptualisation of university teaching excellence' (p. 7). Nowadays HE teaching typically involves a multitude of differing scenarios, sites, interactions and agents, particularly in the case of practice-based courses that incorporate work-based placements and are invariably influenced by the requirements of

Table 4.1. Academic Staff Perceptions of Teaching Excellence.

- *Excellence is subjective and inevitably influenced by students' contributions*
- *'Excellence' involves differentiation and assessment variation*
- *At the heart of excellence is the value of subject knowledge and experience*
- *An excellent teacher should engender excellent learning and engage students' attention*
- *A variety of styles; mindful of students' preferred ways to learn/ engage*
- *Passionate about your subject and being able to transmit that passion to students*
- *Listening to what students want to learn and incorporating this into the course, whilst managing their expectations*
- *'Excellent teaching' uses engaging models such as flipped classroom, Practice-Based Learning and simulation*
- *'Excellent teaching' includes multidisciplinary teams such as inter-professional learning*
- *Students feel that although education may challenge them, they feel supported and safe during that process*
- *Praxis: theory and practice*
- *Excellence changes over time!*
- *Inspiring and transformative*
- *Passion and enthusiasm coupled with a sound grounding of knowledge and a good evidence base*

professional regulatory bodies. Whilst environments and roles inevitably differ across subject specific courses and institutions, it is possible to identify some of the common features of teaching across a range of disciplines and programmes. Table 4.2 seeks to capture some of these indicative features of HE teaching.

Many of the features discussed in Table 4.2 might be considered to come under the broad category of 'procedural' aspects of teaching. But another lens through which many

Table 4.2. Indicative Features of HE Teaching.

Indicative features of HE teaching	Examples/illustrations
Multiple staff-student teaching dynamics	Tutorials, one-to-one support meetings, small groups, seminar groups, lectures
Multiple sites	On site/campus (e.g. lecture theatres, classrooms, IT suites, laboratories, studios); off-site (e.g. colleges, schools, community, work-based placements) and digital/online (e.g. webinars, VLEs, Skype calls)
Multiple educators	University tutors, work-based mentors, community educators, learning support staff, peer support
Multiple learning events	Lectures, seminars, tutorials, conferences, supervisions, work-based placements, research cafes, group study
Multiple relationships	Staff-students, staff-staff, students-students, students-employers
Contextualising knowledge and skills	Application of subject specific knowledge and skills to the practice-based contexts; linking theory and practice
Critical reflection	Critical reflection on practice, professional learning and self-learning
Updating professional knowledge and skills	Keeping abreast of pedagogical, subject and technological developments

teachers view their work is that of the purpose or function of teaching. Over the course of the last two years, I have worked with hundreds of teachers across different sectors (primary and secondary schools, further and adult education colleges and universities). In our discussions about their perceptions of their role as teachers, patterns have emerged that overlap different contexts, yet equally individual interpretations have differed greatly not just within one sector but a single institution. At one end of the continuum there are those who view teaching from a subject-/content-specific perspective and talk about it as being about explaining, communicating and transmitting (subject) knowledge and skills. At the other end of the continuum are those who view it through a more humanistic lens with the personal development of the student as the key focus and thus see their role as more about nurturing and inspiring an inquisitiveness amongst their students. But, of course, many practitioners position themselves somewhere in the middle of that continuum.

In short, whatever particular focus we choose to adopt when discussing teaching, it is clear that we are dealing with a process that is incredibly complex; a process that does not naturally lend itself to being neatly categorised according to an inherently reductive term like 'excellence', as it can only serve to dilute and simplify that complexity rather than attempt to capture or understand it. Although the discussion above has highlighted that there are some core principles or features of effective teaching that may be pertinent to different sites and contexts, creating systems or frameworks to capture evidence of this for the purposes of monitoring and/or measuring this activity is a different matter altogether. This brings us on to discussing current approaches to evidencing teaching excellence in HE, considering how fit for purpose they are and how we might make better use of them to further our understanding.

EVIDENCING TEACHING EXCELLENCE IN HE: TAKING STOCK AND LOOKING AHEAD

The four subsections that follow discuss key sources of data used in HEIs to monitor and measure the quality of teaching and critically reflect on what each source actually reveals about teaching excellence. Some of these include the core metrics used in the TEF, along with other benchmarking data widely used across the sector. Whilst data from the Destination of Leavers of Higher Education (DLHE) are listed as one of the core metrics of the TEF, I have decided not to include them in this discussion as I do not believe they reveal any discernible findings about the quality of HE teaching, nor were they originally designed to serve this particular purpose. As mentioned in the opening chapter, students themselves remain sceptical about the inclusion of the DLHE data in the TEF on the basis that 'graduate employability is not a measure of teaching quality' (Greatbatch & Holland, 2016, p. 6). Arguably, however, the NSS and student feedback in general have a more credible contribution to make to discussions about teaching excellence than the DLHE survey as they provide a platform for students to articulate their views on the perceived impact of teaching on their learning experience, regardless of the flaws associated with data sets like the NSS and the methods used to collect them.

Student Voice and Teaching Quality

Student voice has become a powerful force in HE. Although government policy has increasingly conceptualised and branded students as consumers in recent years, there is a growing bank of research across education sectors that highlights the important contribution that student consultation can make to bringing about improvements to teaching quality. For example, Niemi, Heikkinen, and Kannas (2010) argue that 'involving students ... in educational decision-making, and listening seriously to their stories of experiences as learners [are] essential first steps in developing education' (2010, p. 139). Similarly, Healey, Flint, and Harrington (2014) put forward a strong case for student engagement and building partnerships between staff and students where both parties stand to gain from reciprocal learning.

In the current marketised climate, the influence of student voice on HE policy and decision making continues to grow, which means that HEIs have to consider carefully how they engage with and respond to their students. Ever since the advent of the National Student Survey (NSS)[1] in 2005, its stock value has risen rapidly. With the subsequent introduction of higher tuition fees and the reduction in HEFCE funding, universities have come to attach greater importance to the results of the NSS. So concerned are some HEIs with maximising NSS response rates that they have created specific posts to reinforce its importance and the need for students to complete it. Furthermore, the current minister of state for universities and science, Jo Johnson, declared that one of the reasons for the need to introduce the TEF was because of the perceived decline in student satisfaction scores, continuing the prioritisation of student satisfaction above all else as a proxy for teaching quality epitomised in the Browne review of HE (2010) that identified student choice as the key driver for improvement. Yet HEFCE's own review of the NSS, which was carried out in 2016, contradicted the government's claims of a decline, instead revealing a steady increase in student satisfaction score with the overall satisfaction at 87% (HEFCE, 2016).

Whilst universities and student bodies have focused a lot of attention on marketing and promoting the NSS to date, less attention has been given to how best to engage students with the process of evaluation and the evidence they draw on to ensure that their responses are suitably informed and represent a balanced and accurate reflection of their university experiences. The National Union of Students has acknowledged that many students neglect the survey, largely because they do not realise the significance and impact of their responses. Student leaders have therefore concentrated on raising awareness, with a view to maximising response rates as results are only published for those courses where the response rate hits the minimum threshold of 50%. But, in the context of the TEF, it inevitably raises the question of how well-equipped students are to comment on aspects of pedagogic and subject knowledge expertise. How do we know, for example, that their responses are not based on superficial and arbitrary criteria such as the lecturer's personality and whether or not they like them rather than an informed understanding of subject knowledge or learning and teaching as a whole?

One of the criticisms of the NSS is that it stifles and even penalises innovative and challenging teaching, with some studies suggesting that students report greater satisfaction rates on courses where they are less likely to be taken out of their comfort zone and exposed to teaching and assessments that challenge them or get them to take risks (e.g. Poropat, 2014). In an increasingly competitive market and given the financial commitment associated with university study nowadays, it is perhaps unsurprising that students may seek to minimise risk to the outcome of what has undoubtedly become a high-stakes assessment, i.e. their final degree classification. Yet ironically, when it comes to teaching excellence, innovation and experimentation are commonly acknowledged as key features (e.g. Gunn and Fisk, 2013). Besides, being challenged and unsettled in one's thinking has traditionally been a distinctive quality of university education, as Barnett (1990) reminds us:

> *A genuine higher learning is subversive in the sense of subverting the student's taken-for-granted world, including the world of endeavour, scholarship, calculation or creativity, into which he or she has been initiated. A genuine higher education is unsettling; it is not meant to be a cosy experience. It is disturbing because, ultimately, the student comes to see that things could always be other than they are. (p. 155)*

Understandably students are key agents in the learning and teaching process and as such have an important contribution to make in sharing their views about their learning experiences, but the extent to which they can be expected to produce a fair, valid and reliable assessment of the quality of teaching is an important issue that needs to be unearthed more thoroughly in HEIs. Recent research into the use of classroom observation in post-compulsory education settings, for example, has highlighted how difficult it is even for the most highly experienced observers working with tried and tested assessment criteria over a sustained period of time to make valid and reliable assessments of teaching (e.g. O'Leary, 2013; O'Leary & Wood, 2016). This is an area that is discussed in greater detail below but suffice to say that there are interesting parallels between the role of students as respondents of their learning experience and that of academic staff evaluating teaching.

Professor Chris Husbands, the first chair of the TEF assessment panel has openly stated that he '[does] not think student satisfaction is an accurate proxy for teaching quality' and that NSS scores 'will have only a limited impact' on the overall assessment and subsequent grading of institutions, although he refused to discount them from the assessment framework (Grove, 2017). I agree with Husbands to the extent that student satisfaction per se cannot and should not be regarded as an 'accurate proxy for teaching quality' but at the same time student voice is integral to developing a more enlightened understanding of the learning–teaching interface, regardless of policy agendas like the TEF and the political motives for such initiatives. Thus it is not a case of *should* students play a part in informing current thinking and practice but *how* they should do so and how best academics might work in partnership with them.

There is a need for more transparent dialogue amongst HEI staff and students as to what the nature and purpose of the NSS are, why it is important to gather feedback on their experiences and the impact of that data on the experiences of future students. Both parties need to approach the process as a catalyst for generating meaningful, reciprocal discussion about wider issues relating to the students' engagement with and reaction to their teaching and how this impacts on the student learning experience as a whole.

The first part of the NSS asks students about the quality of teaching, assessment and feedback. Surely these are aspects of practice that students and staff need to be engaged in ongoing discussions about throughout the course? Starting a dialogue with students from the beginning of their course about teaching, assessment and feedback is crucial to developing an understanding of their learning experiences and in turn building a partnership between the two key protagonists involved in the interrelated processes of learning and teaching.

To stimulate initial discussion, lecturers could start by giving their students an insight into why they choose to employ particular teaching styles or what they consider to be the most effective ways of providing feedback. This should not be presented in a vacuum purely to prepare students for the

NSS, but should be embedded into live courses so that the discussion is put into context and resonates with students. For example, we could ask students what they think about the assessment methods used on their course. Are they an effective means of testing and developing their knowledge, understanding and skills? What do they think about the quality of the feedback they receive? What do they do with that feedback and does it help to further their understanding? As part of such discussion, students should be given the opportunity to put forward their opinions, ask questions and seek clarification with a view to them feeling a genuine sense of inclusion in the ongoing development of the curriculum.

This type of open, reciprocal dialogue between staff and students is fundamental. Without it universities risk students basing their responses to the NSS or any other survey on teaching not on an informed understanding of the complex decision-making processes that teaching staff invariably undergo when planning, delivering and assessing a programme of study, but on a hunch or an individual preference. As we shall see below when discussing teaching observations, this can equally be used for lecturers to reflect on their own practice both with their peers and students. For example, do they have a particular philosophy of learning and teaching? How does this impact on the way they plan, deliver and evaluate their own teaching? Are they aware of how effective their teaching is? How do they monitor this?

Students undoubtedly have a vital role to play in contributing to a greater understanding of and helping to bring about improvements in the quality of HE teaching. Whether it be the representation of their voices collectively as part of large data sets such as the NSS or their individual feedback to staff, students are key agents in the teaching–learning relationship. Nevertheless, it is important to make sure that opinions about the student experience as a whole are not confused and/or conflated with the quality of teaching as a particular element of their wider HE experience, which is a criticism levelled at generic surveys like the NSS.

Students' HE experience extends much further than simply the teaching they experience on their course. Wider institutional services, support systems, communities, cultures and indeed ethos all contribute to students' perceptions of their HE experience. Besides, most students are taught by a multitude of different academic staff during their course, which makes it very difficult to separate out and evaluate the impact that individual staff or specific modules may have had on their overall outcomes and/or their learning experience. Although the NSS is not sophisticated enough to capture information at programme and modular level, it can act as a catalyst for conversations between students and staff within individual HEIs about their shared experiences of learning and teaching. Rather than seeing it as an exercise in which students respond as passive consumers, engaging students in critical reflection and active dialogue with their peers and lecturers from early on in their courses has the potential to transform their views of how valuable and meaningful student voice can be to both parties.

Student Outcomes and Teaching Quality

Student record data collected by the Higher Education Statistics Agency form one of the core metrics of the TEF. This is hardly surprising as data relating to recruitment, retention, progression and attainment have been used for monitoring and measuring the quality of educational provision across sectors for some time. But the extent to which the quality of teaching in particular can be seen to impact directly on these outcomes remains highly contestable and controversial. As Gibbs (2015) has commented, 'outcome measures are strongly influenced by a raft of variables that tell us nothing about institutional quality'.

The dominant policy discourse in schools and colleges in recent years has been one that has sought to reinforce the link between teaching and educational outcomes, as though teaching were the only variable that matters and anything else is extraneous. Agencies aligned with the state, such as the Office for Standards in Education (Ofsted), have played a key role in driving this agenda, as indeed has the wider 'evidence-based' movement in education that has gained considerable traction in the schools' sector in the United Kingdom and the United States over the last decade. Although it is beyond the scope of this chapter to discuss evidence-based education in any detail, it is important to recognise its influence on education policy and practice (see Biesta, 2007 for further discussion). The positivist positionality of evidence-based practice conceptualises teaching and learning as a scientific process with observable and measurable correlations between the input (teaching) and output (learning), but disregards the importance of other factors (e.g. cultural, economic, social) in understanding the relationship between the two. Yet this is despite the fact that a substantial body of research has identified social class and cultural capital as significant variables that impact on educational attainment (e.g. De Graaf, De Graaf, & Kraaykamp, 2000; Sullivan, 2001).

In the case of student recruitment and retention, HEIs that are highly selective clearly have a distinct advantage over those that recruit from a wider community. The main reasons why students withdraw from courses are invariably related to matters other than the quality of teaching or other academic issues. Furthermore, students from working class backgrounds tend to be more affected by such matters than their counterparts from (upper) middle class backgrounds, often because they have to contend with a multitude of extracurricular commitments, pressures and the challenges of cultural assimilation as well as their studies (e.g. Quinn, 2004). Thus, when it comes to these data being used for comparative statistical analyses across HEIs for the purpose of exercises like the TEF, as Holmwood, Hickey, Cohen, and Wallis (2016, p. 29) assert, 'universities with a strong widening participation track record will inevitably suffer … [as they] face being blamed for forces beyond their control'.

In the case of student attainment, the raw completion data only capture achievement at the end point of the programme of study, thus, once again, for HEIs with a significant widening participation student population, no account is taken of the distance travelled from their point of entry or the value added. But surely this is a valuable variable to include in the context of teaching excellence and the wider issue of student support? The transformational impact that a university education can have on the lives of students from less affluent and privileged backgrounds may not necessarily be captured in attainment data but that does not make it any less real or valuable for those students themselves.

A further shortcoming in using student attainment as a measurement of teaching quality is that it can run the risk of shifting responsibility for the final outcome from students to lecturers, thus reinforcing the conceptualisation of students as passive consumers rather than as active partners in their learning experience. In turn this can reconfigure notions of accountability in such a way that student failure can be attributed to academic staff rather than the students themselves. This goes against the grain of the ethos and mission of HE insomuch as it is underpinned by collaborative and reciprocal relationships between academic staff and students, both of whom play their own vital role in shaping the outcomes of the teaching–learning relationship.

HEA Fellowship

One of the most popular and widely embraced means of recognising and accrediting excellence in professional practice and leadership in teaching and learning in UK universities in recent years is the Higher Education Academy's (HEA) fellowship scheme. The HEA was established in 2003 to provide an accreditation scheme for university teachers in the United Kingdom and in doing so it created its United Kingdom Professional Standards Framework (UKPSF), a set of standards and national benchmarking tool designed to outline the main dimensions of the teaching and learning support roles that exist within HE.

According to its chief executive, the HEA is the 'HE sector champion of teaching quality' (Marshall, 2015), with its fellowship scheme aligned with the UKPSF, HEA fellowships offer four levels of accreditation: (1) associate fellow; (2) fellow; (3) senior fellow and (4) principal fellow. With over 86,000 individual fellows registered worldwide as of March 2017 (HEA, 2017), HEA fellowships have increasingly come to be seen by some as an important proxy for recognition of teaching competence and effectiveness. Yet the extent to which HEA fellowships can be considered a valid and/or reliable indicator of teaching quality is a matter of some debate.

Firstly, there is the issue of the methodology of the assessment and conferment of fellowship status to consider. In essence, HEA fellowships are a desk-based, paper exercise that are largely reliant on the self-narratives and supporting evidence provided by the applicants themselves. Individual applicants are required to complete a written application that demonstrates how they have achieved each of the descriptors for their respective level, along with a supporting statement(s) from other HE professionals. These applications are then evaluated by a group of accredited assessors who decide whether the evidence presented in the application successfully meets the established criteria, with the final decision ratified by a confirmation panel. Thus the decision to award fellowship is ostensibly based on the ability of the applicant to present a convincing written case of their professional practice, knowledge, skills and values. In this sense it could be argued that the process is as much about the applicant's proficiency in literary expression as it is about demonstrating tangible evidence of excellence in teaching.

From an assessment perspective, there are also questions to consider concerning the validity and reliability of the process. Validity refers to the notion of an assessment actually assessing what it purports to assess. Reliability refers to the consistency and replicability of the assessment results. Thus in relation to the HEA fellowship scheme, the most obvious question concerning validity centres on the extent to which a written form of assessment can be regarded as a suitable and credible representation of one's teaching expertise. Or to think of it another way, if we wanted to assess a student nurse's ability to take a patient's blood pressure, would asking them to write an essay on the subject be the most appropriate method of assessment?

Secondly, given that the HEA fellowship scheme was originally created with a focus on learning and teaching and the accreditation of HE teachers, it is interesting to note that the most senior level of recognition (principal fellow) is saved for those who invariably occupy the roles of senior leadership and management in HE. In the previous chapter, Phil Wood used the term 'codification of excellence' to refer to the fellowship scheme. What is clear about the HEA's scheme is that it enshrines a hierarchy of excellence in which strategic leadership is valued more highly over teaching, at least in terms of its recognition and accompanying status. This may also explain then the HEA's role in shaping the TEF framework and the decision to create an accreditation model based on a gold, silver, bronze award system, which seems to have originated from a proposal by the HEA itself as its chief executive reported in October 2015 (Marshall, 2015) prior to the publication of the HE White Paper in May of 2016.

The HEA fellowship may very well have been conceived and created with the best intentions of raising the profile and ensuring greater recognition of learning and teaching in the sector. The reality is, however, that it has increasingly been appropriated as a competency-based, tick-box exercise with many HEIs adopting a blanket policy to push all academic staff to acquire their fellowship in light of the TEF. The extent to which participation in the process and the award of fellowship status to individuals captures teaching excellence or indeed has a tangible impact on the quality of learning and teaching and the student learning experience in the institution as a whole remains unclear. Another contributory factor to this may be the individualistic conceptualisation of teaching encapsulated in the scheme. To echo Phil Wood's thoughts in the previous chapter, focusing on the 'I' rather than the 'we' results in excellence becoming a competitive tool rather than a collaborative signifier.

Observations and Teaching Quality

Classroom observation has long occupied a prominent place in the formal assessment and development of teachers in colleges and schools in the United Kingdom. In contrast, its use in HE has been less commonplace, with practice much more sporadic across the sector. However, with teaching excellence now firmly in the policy spotlight with the TEF, observation is increasingly being employed as a quality assurance tool to gather information on teaching standards and to evidence staff performance across HE. But what lessons can be learnt about its use elsewhere?

In colleges and schools, observation has come to be relied upon as the main source of evidence for judging the professional capabilities of teachers in recent years, both internally for employers and externally for government agencies. Its use has largely been driven by a performance management agenda, which has culminated in the creation and overreliance on a set of reductive metrics and practices to judge the overall quality of teaching and learning, typified by the categorisation of teachers' performance in observations against some form of ranking scale (see, e.g. O'Leary, 2014).

Recent research on the use and impact of observation in further education in England has called into question the efficacy of using it as a performance indicator, arguing that such models are invariably underpinned by a managerialist, marketised agenda that fails to create an authentic, meaningful learning and teaching environment for students and staff alike (e.g. O'Leary, 2013; O'Leary & Wood, 2016). The findings from a large-scale study revealed that teachers regarded performance management, assessment-based models of observation as of little relevance to their professional needs. There was a consensus that such models of observation failed to improve their teaching and were often a deterrent to developing innovations in practice. In contrast, the overwhelming majority of participants agreed that low-stakes, peer-based models of observation were most conducive to sustainable change and professional learning and thus should be at the forefront of providers' use of observation and wider professional development strategy (UCU, 2013). Thus there are valuable lessons for HE to learn from colleges and schools regarding the effective use of observation.

Emergent findings from an ongoing HEFCE-funded project at Birmingham City University[2] reinforce the value of removing observation from the context of assessment, revealing how it can create a safe, low-stakes environment for reflection and dialogue between academic staff and students. At the same time, this has also opened up new opportunities for the way in which observation can be used as a lens for informing understanding of effective learning and teaching.

The primary aim of the project has been to create an authentic and sustainable collaboration between academic staff and students using observation as a central reference point and a tool for critical inquiry into learning and teaching, empowering students to play an active role in shaping their learning experience. The project reconceptualises and reconfigures the use of observation as a method to enhance learning and teaching. It repositions it from being a performance management mechanism to a collaborative method of inquiry in which students and lecturers co-interrogate and co-reflect on their own and each other's learning and teaching values and practices, with a view to reciprocally enhancing their shared experiences. Crucially, the involvement of students as co-observers, co reflectors and co-researchers reconceptualises their identity from consumers and evaluators of their learning experience to co-enquirers and co-producers of knowledge about HE learning and teaching.

In contrast to conventional models of observation that focus on the performance of the individual lecturer, the project adopts a holistic, case study approach, drawing on different sources of evidence and methods to create a richer, more triangulated understanding of practice. By involving students and staff as co-researchers and co-reflectors, a greater awareness and transparency about the effectiveness of current practices have emerged. Involving students and staff co-observing and discussing pedagogical practices have also opened up the opportunity to build a community where students and staff collaborate on programme planning, delivery and evaluation.

In this sense, observation has provided a shared reference point, which has acted as a catalyst for academic staff and students to engage in dialogic interaction about their perceptions of learning and teaching and in so doing, reinforcing the importance of collaborative inquiry. As Greatbatch and Holland (2016) found in their recent study:

> *Research shows the importance of considering the micro-processes surrounding teaching and learning such as lecturers' teaching strategies and the characteristics of university students' learning. (2016, p. 4)*

CONCLUDING REMARKS

The ever-increasing marketisation and commodification of HE have given rise to a dominant discourse or what Green (2011) refers to as 'managerialese'. It is a neoliberal discourse of the market underpinned by an ideology that sees businesses (i.e. HEIs) as the providers of a service to their customers/service users (i.e. students). The very term 'teaching excellence' is an extension of that managerialist discourse, a marketised misconception of the complex reality of the reciprocal relationship between teaching and learning, and between staff and students; a relationship that is characterised by collective collaboration not individualistic one-upmanship. As remarked in the previous chapter, one of the consequences of competitive schemes like the TEF is that they accentuate the importance of the individual over the collective, thus eschewing the value of collegiality and collaboration in teaching. However, the collaborative observation project discussed in this chapter highlights the importance of seeing students as partners not products in a reciprocal endeavour and the gains that can be made for both parties in doing so.

Conceptualising education as a process of 'production' in which students are the 'products' inevitably results in the adoption of a reductionist lens, where the complexity of the iterative relationships of teaching and learning is ignored. Furthermore, this reductionist approach sees teaching and learning as a form of instrumentalist technology in which the means can be controlled and manipulated to bring about the desired ends. Or in this case, establish what needs to be taught (the curriculum), identify the most effective means of teaching (pedagogy) and learning (theories of learning) and the desired outcomes will be achieved.

Teaching is not a mechanical process involving the application of a prescribed set of approaches or techniques in order to achieve predetermined outcomes; it is a complex art that is constantly evolving. The reason for that is simple and rooted in the complexity of human beings and the sometimes unpredictable and uncontrollable way in which they behave and interact. As Ramsden and Callender (2014) point out:

> *Students on a course experience the same teaching and the same course, but they experience them in different ways. Becoming aware of those differences, and trying to understand them, is the key to improving students' experiences of learning. (p. 41)*

How any given student interprets information presented to them by a teacher and what they then choose to do with that information is largely dependent on: (1) how the teacher chooses to present and communicate the information and (2) how each learner makes sense of the experience. Thus there is a reciprocal filter at play in the relationship between teaching (input) and learning (output) which makes it very difficult for either party to anticipate and to prepare for with a high degree of certainty, despite what evidence-based approaches to education might have us believe.

Regardless of where and what students choose to study, their HE learning experience is inevitably determined by a range of factors, of which the quality of teaching is only one. There are many other economic, social and cultural factors that impact on their experience so any tool for assessing quality and identifying excellence needs to take account of these different and complex variables before an authentic and meaningful judgement can be made about the quality of teaching in any HEI. Whether the current TEF is designed or indeed is capable of doing this remains a moot point, but this should not stop everyone with an interest in HE from continuing to strive for a framework that is fair and equitable.

It is too early yet to know whether the TEF and the current focus on the quality of teaching will have a tangible and/or lasting impact on learning and teaching across HE or simply turn out to be a reform that results in the creation of new layers of accountability initiatives and QA mechanisms. What we do know, however, is that there are valuable lessons for the HE sector to learn from the schools' improvement agenda about the counterproductive effects of relying too heavily on the use of metrics to assess and performance manage educational provision. We need to focus less on publicly identifying excellence and more on understanding and developing effective and authentic practice. Whilst recognition and reward schemes may act as short-term incentives, there is little evidence that they lead to long-term, sustainable improvement either individually or institutionally. This is something that comes from supporting not sorting staff. Ultimately, the most meaningful and sustainable indicators of the quality of teaching do not come from external inspection of validation, but through the nurturing of an institution's staff, along with a commitment on the part of those staff to want to continuously reflect and improve on what they do.

NOTES

1. The NSS is a survey of all final-year degree students at institutions in England, Wales and Northern Ireland. The survey is designed to assess students' opinions of the quality of their degree programmes, with seven different scores published including an 'overall satisfaction' mark.

2. *Improving learning and teaching through collaborative observation* is an 18-month project funded by the Higher Education Funding Council for England taking place in the Faculty of Health, Education and Life Sciences at Birmingham City University from November 2016 to April 2018. The project consists of five case studies from different subject areas across the faculty.

REFERENCES

Barnett, R. (1990). *The idea of higher education*. Buckingham: Open University Press.

Biesta, G. (2007). Why 'what works' won't work: Evidence-based practice and the democratic deficit in educational research. *Educational Theory*, *57*(1), 1–22.

Browne, J. (2010). *Securing a sustainable future in higher education*. Department of Business Innovation and Skills, London. Retrieved from www.bis.gov.uk/assets/biscore/corporate/docs/s/10-1208-securing-sustainable-higher-education-brownereport.pdf. Accessed on November 21, 2016.

Collini, S. (2012). *What are universities for?* London: Penguin.

De Graaf, N. D., De Graaf, P. M., & Kraaykamp, G. (2000). Parental cultural capital and educational attainment in the Netherlands: A refinement of the cultural capital perspective. *Sociology of Education*, *73*, 92–111.

Department for Business, Innovation and Skills. (2016). *Success as a knowledge economy: Teaching excellence, social mobility and student choice*. Higher Education White Paper.

Gibbs, G. (2015). Graduate employability data no way to measure teaching quality. *Times Higher Education*, Article published online July 7, 2015. Retrieved from https://www.timeshighereducation.com/blog/graduate-employability-data-no-way-measure-teaching-quality. Accessed on May 21, 2017.

Gill, J. (2015). David Willetts interview: 'What I did was in the interests of young people'. *Times Higher Education*, Article published online June 18, 2015. Retrieved from https://www.timeshighereducation.com/david-willetts-what-i-did-was-in-the-interests-of-young-people. Accessed on May 4, 2017.

Greatbatch, D., & Holland, J. (2016, May). *Teaching quality in higher education: Literature review and qualitative research*. Department for Business, Innovation and Skills.

Green, J. (2011). *Education, professionalism and the quest for accountability*. New York, NY: Routledge.

Grove, J. (2017). TEF to limit use of 'flawed' NSS scores. *Times Higher Education*, Article published online January 25, 2017. Retrieved from https://www.timeshighereducation.

com/news/tef-limit-use-flawed-nss-scores#node-comments. Accessed on May 14, 2017.

Gunn, V., & Fisk, A. (2013). *Considering teaching excellence in higher education 2007-2013: A Literature Review since the CHERI Report 2007*. Higher Education Academy, York, UK.

(HEA) Higher Education Academy Fellowship – Online (2017). Retrieved from https://www.heacademy.ac.uk/individuals/fellowship?utm_source=Google%20(Grant)&utm_medium=PPC&utm_campaign=Professional%20Practice%20-%20Fellowship&gclid=CjwKEAjw2qzHBRChloWxgoXDpyASJAB01Io0dTZ2hpqHIkdqi57rNjseituKMzr-oOu5bzOoL9Z_FRoCpJrw_wcB. Accessed on April 6, 2017.

Healey, M., Flint, A., & Harrington, K. (2014). *Engagement through partnership: Students as partners in learning and teaching in higher education*. York: HEA. Retrieved from https://www.heacademy.ac.uk/engagement-through-partnership-students-partners-learningand-teaching-higher-education. Accessed on May 21, 2017.

HEFCE. (2016). *National Student Survey*. Retrieved from http://www.hefce.ac.uk/lt/nss. Accessed on May 14, 2017.

Holmwood, J., Hickey, T., Cohen, R., & Wallis, S. (2016). In defence of public higher education: Knowledge for a successful society. A response to 'Success as a Knowledge Economy', BIS (2016). *Convention for Higher Education*.

Husbands, C., & Pearce, J. (2012). *What makes great pedagogy? Nine claims from research*. Nottingham, NCSL. Retrieved from https://www.gov.uk/government/uploads/system/uploads/attachment_data/file/329746/what-makes-great-pedagogy-nine-claims-from-research.pdf. Accessed on May 11, 2017.

James, M., & Pollard, A. (2011). TLRP's ten principles for effective pedagogy: Rationale, development, evidence, argument and impact. *Research Papers in Education*, *26*(3), 275–328.

Marshall, S. (2015). Proposing a sustainable Teaching Excellence Framework. *WONKHE*, Published online October 5, 2015. Retrieved from http://wonkhe.com/blogs/proposing-a-sustainable-teaching-excellence-framework/. Accessed on April 12, 2017.

Niemi, R., Heikkinen, H. L. T., & Kannas, L. (2010). Polyphony in the classroom: Reporting narrative action research reflexively. *Educational Action Research*, *18*(2), 137–149.

O'Leary, M. (2013). Surveillance, performativity and normalised practice: The use and impact of graded lesson observations in Further Education Colleges. *Journal of Further and Higher Education*, *37*(5), 694–714.

O'Leary, M. (2014). *Classroom observation: A guide to the effective observation of teaching and learning*. London: Routledge.

O'Leary, M., & Wood, P. (2016). Performance over professional learning and the complexity puzzle: Lesson observation in England's further education sector. *Professional Development in Education*. Retrieved from http://dx.doi.org/10.1080/19415257.2016.1210665. Accessed on December 19, 2016.

Poropat, A. (2014). Students don't know what's best for their own learning. *The Conversation*, November 18. Retrieved from https://theconversation.com/students-dont-know-whats-best-for-theirown-learning-33835. Accessed on May 20, 2017.

Quinn, J. (2004). Understanding working-class 'drop-out' from higher education through a sociocultural lens: Cultural narratives and local contexts. *International Studies in Sociology of Education*, *14*(1), 57–74.

Ramsden, P., & Callender, C. (2014). *Appendix A: Literature review*. Retrieved from http://www.hefce.ac.uk/media/fb/content/pubs/indirreports/2014/Review,of,the,NSS/2014_nssreviewa.pdf. Accessed on October 23, 2016.

Skelton, A. (2004). Understanding teaching excellence in higher education: A critical evaluation of the national teaching fellowships scheme. *Studies in Higher Education*, *29*(4), 451–468.

Sullivan, A. (2001). Cultural capital and educational attainment. *Sociology*, *34*(4), 893–912.

University and College Union (UCU). (2013). *Developing a national framework for the effective use of lesson observation in further education*. Project Report for University and College Union, November 2013. Retrieved from http://www.ucu.org.uk/7105. Accessed on October 25, 2016.

5

DEVELOPING AND SUPPORTING TEACHING EXCELLENCE IN HIGHER EDUCATION

Sue Robson

INTRODUCTION

Academic work has changed significantly in recent decades, as universities worldwide respond to globalisation, the massification of higher education (HE) and the increasing demands placed upon them by their national governments. New public management and neoliberalism have become powerful political drivers of a quality culture in HE across the world (Behari-Leak, 2017; Deem, Hillyard, & Reed, 2007; Enders & de Weert, 2009; Hénard, 2010) as discussed in Chapter 2. Governments have sought to exercise greater control over universities' activities by introducing initiatives to evaluate the quality of their investments (Weir, 2009). Research and innovation are key quality dimensions linked to economic development that have underpinned successive HE reforms and the more widespread occurrence of excellence initiatives in HE (OECD, 2015; Pruvot & Estermann, 2014). However, research as one important mission of HE has perhaps overshadowed an equally important core mission of HE: teaching and learning (McAleese, 2013).

The UK Research Excellence Framework (REF) (http://www.ref.ac.uk/) and the German Exzellenz Initiativ (DFG, 2013) are examples of systems for the evaluation of research quality that are powerful determinants of institutional status (Brusoni et al., 2014). In a competitive environment encouraged by league tables and rankings (e.g. QS World University Rankings; Times Higher Education World University Rankings), research excellence is central to a prestige culture that influences which institutions can recruit the best students and world-leading staff from an international market (Blackmore, Blackwell, & Edmondson, 2016; Forstenzer, 2016). Given the prestige afforded to research excellence, teaching excellence has been perceived as less important in many HE institutions (Brew, 2012; Cashmore & Ramsden, 2009a, ,2009b; MacKenzie & Robertson, 2009). This is particularly the case at more senior academic levels. The report on excellent education in research-rich universities by Fung, Besters-Dilger, and van der Vaart (2017, p. 7), for the League of European Research Universities, noted that education-focused leadership has 'had less favourable conditions for reward and promotion' in these institutions. This concern was borne out by Gunn and Fisk (2013) in their review of the literature on teaching excellence, which found that teaching leadership tends not to be recognised in promotions. This may leave staff with teaching-focused careers feeling undervalued and demotivated.

This chapter seeks to address the recognition, support and development needs of teaching-focused academics. It considers the complexities of teaching and educational leadership roles and the need for recognition of different forms of teaching excellence across the academic career profile. It suggests the importance of collaborative forms of professional development and engagement to promote in teaching-focused academics a sense of belonging to a valued university community; to promote greater reflectivity, review of habitual practices and openness to new theoretical and pedagogical perspectives; and to support the collation of evidence of what is excellent in teaching across a range of career phases and profiles.

RECOGNISING AND REWARDING TEACHING EXCELLENCE

Excellence 'is an emotive, if familiar, word in HE, but its pursuit is permeated by socio-cultural characteristics such as gender and ethnicity' (Deem, 2015, p. 4). Female academics, for instance, have voiced concerns that selection processes for senior posts tend to focus on rather narrow sets of achievements, such as awards received and papers written, whereas the teaching, administration and outreach work in which many women excel are not sufficiently valued (Jarboe, 2016). Jarboe (2016, p. 49) cites Professor Dame Athene Donald, Professor of Experimental Physics, who suggests the need to appropriately *reward and embed different types of success, such as teaching, outreach and departmental support; activities that ... are not currently a meaningful part of recognition and advancement in universities.*

Data from the UK (HESA, 2015–2016) indicating that while women make up 47% of the academic workforce, only 23% of professors are women supports these concerns. Similarly, in Europe only 18% of full professorships are held by women (Vernos, 2013), while reports from America and

Australia also indicate that women hold fewer senior posts than men (Deem, 2015). A note of optimism is, however, evident in that 'committed and collective action to increase women's leadership' has begun by the HE funding bodies, sector umbrella bodies and individual HE institutions (Jarboe, 2016, p. 4).

The status of teaching and the reward and recognition of teaching and teaching leadership have become national policy issues for HE (MacKenzie & Robertson, 2009). This is evident in the fact that quality assurance (QA) initiatives for research excellence (REF) are now mirrored in the Teaching Excellence Framework (TEF) initiatives for teaching. The adoption of revised *Standards and guidelines for quality assurance in the European higher education area* (2015) and beyond have been presented as a means to address the perceived imbalance between teaching and research and to reward excellent teaching in HE. Initiatives in countries worldwide, including South Africa (Leibowitz, Farmer, & Franklin, 2012; Searle & McKenna, 2013); Finland (Finnish Higher Education Evaluation Council – FINHEEC); the Netherlands (Accreditation Organisation of the Netherlands and Flanders – NVAO); Australia (the Australian Government Office for Learning and Teaching); and New Zealand (New Zealand Universities Academic Audit Unit) have introduced quality measures for HE teaching (Dittrich in Brusoni et al., 2014). The introduction of a TEF has been presented as a means 'to recognise and reward excellent teaching in UK HE providers' (HEFCE, 2017).

Attempts to reward good teaching are welcome (Gibbs, 2016). However, when 'discourses of neoliberalism intersect with teaching and learning practices' (Burke, Stevenson, & Whelan, 2015, p. 29), the stated intentions to rebalance the ways in which teaching is regarded compared with research are met with a degree of scepticism (Cashmore, 2009a; Weir,

2009). There is little empirical evidence to indicate that quality measures employed by TEF capture the complexity of teaching excellence demonstrated across institutions and cultural contexts, disciplines and programmes, and by individual or collaborative teams of academics (Schindler, Puls-Elvidge, Welzant, & Crawford, 2015; Skelton, 2004). The 'normative universalising of teaching excellence' (Greatbatch & Holland, 2016, p. 11) has been criticised for reifying systems over the development of strong values and cultures of teaching (Searle & McKenna, 2013). There are concerns that the real aim of external quality audits is to make universities more accountable rather than to enhance the quality of learning and teaching (Searle & McKenna, *ibid.*).

Some studies suggest that a combination of external audit and internal university processes can stimulate change and improvement in teaching (Greatbatch & Holland, 2016). Beckmann (2016, p. 1), however, questions whether approaches that are in essence both competitive and comparative, and focus on the few that can demonstrate the 'elusive trait of excellence', actually 'divide more than they unite'. This can lead to performative cultures and an intensification of competition and individualism in the quest for recognition and reward rather than valuing collegiality (Weir, 2009).

Comparison of practices can be productive, however, when it is used to develop, recognise and reward teaching excellence at all levels, to identify and share effective practices and to incorporate them in resources and initiatives that can help to facilitate change (Wills, 2010, cited in HEA, 2013b). The international *Promoting Teaching* Project (HEA, 2013a, 2013b) sought to support the development of a quality culture for teaching by drawing on expertise and innovative practice examples from Australia and the United Kingdom to produce such resources (this initiative and its outputs will be referred to in more detail later in the chapter).

Responding to concerns within the sector, mechanisms to support, recognise and celebrate excellent teaching at institutional, national and global levels have been developed (Brusoni et al., 2014; Fung et al., 2017). Organisations such as the Higher Education Academy (HEA) in the United Kingdom have devised awards to recognise and reward individual excellence (National Teaching Fellowships), collaborative teamwork (Collaborative Awards for Teaching Excellence, 2016) and institutional excellence (The Global Teaching Excellence Award, introduced in 2017). The Global Teaching Excellence Award is thought to be the first HE award of its kind to recognise commitment to teaching that is considered to be world-class, in terms of the leadership of teaching, students' learning and student support (HEA, 2017).

A number of universities have also developed internal methods and mechanisms to acknowledge the contribution of academics to teaching excellence, although there is as yet a lack of convincing evidence that they are being systematically used and valued (Cashmore, Cane, Cane, & Stainton, 2013; HEA, 2013b; Mackenzie & Robertson, 2009). More development work is needed to communicate and build on policy initiatives, to address the perceived status of teaching excellence compared to research excellence, to grow and develop excellent 'communities of leader-scholars, willing and able to learn and tackle together the challenges of contemporary academic life' (Hill, p. 30) and to build a quality culture around teaching (Fung et al., 2017).

REFINING NOTIONS OF TEACHING EXCELLENCE

Challenging the normative notions of teaching excellence that permeate quality audit criteria and frameworks is problematic, especially, when there is no consensus on a more acceptable definition of excellence (Bråten, 2014; Greatbatch & Holland, 2016; Land & Gordon, 2015). A challenge for the sector is to consider how best to respond to the particular conceptualisation of teaching excellence permeating TEF and HERB (see Chapter 2 for more detailed discussion).

The widespread 'lack of sophistication in conceptualisation of university teaching excellence' (Gunn & Fisk, 2013, p. 7), particularly in terms of how the academic role may change over the course of a career, needs to be addressed. The development of a dialogue to refine understandings of what is 'necessary', what is 'good' and what is 'excellent' in university teaching, can lead to more nuanced conceptions of teaching excellence that may help institutions to recognise the multidimensional and dynamic nature of teaching (Quinlan, 2014; van Lankveld et al., 2016; Gibbs, 2016; Forstenzer, 2016), as discussed in the preceding chapters. Recognition of threshold, good and excellent teaching requires that the nature and mix of evidence will vary across a range of academic career profiles, to show development over time and demonstrate relevance according to context, for example, in teaching or research-focused institutions (Australian Learning & Teaching Council, 2009; Cashmore et al., 2009a, 2009b; Gunn & Fisk, 2013; Law, 2011; Locke, Whitchurch, Smith, & Mazenod, 2016; Probert, 2013). The contribution to excellence of education leaders, of teachers with sophisticated, research-informed professional beliefs, identities and practices, and of innovative, collaborative teaching teams should not be overlooked (Blackmore et al., 2016; Fung et al., 2017; Searle & McKenna, 2013; Stevenson, Burke, & Whelan, 2014).

PROFESSIONAL LEARNING AND TEACHING EXCELLENCE

In parallel with mechanisms for the reward and recognition of teaching excellence, professional learning and development initiatives are important to help teaching-focused academics to feel supported and valued (Van Lankveld et al., 2016). Providing opportunities to reflect upon the ways in which teaching has developed in response to academic, social, economic and political challenges can help colleagues to construct an evidence base for pedagogical development and innovation. With widening participation, technologisation, internationalisation and the growth of transnational education, come opportunities to demonstrate excellence through innovative, inclusive, culturally sensitive teaching. Raising aspirations, providing students with different cultural perspectives, improving interactions between students, developing their leadership and intercultural skills (Leask, 2009; Mak, Daly, & Barker, 2014) and their responsible use of technologies is important in readiness for the world of work and, perhaps more importantly, to encourage socially responsible citizenship (Clifford & Montgomery, 2014; Reid & Spencer-Oatey, 2013, cited in Robson, 2015).

Teaching-focused academics may take for granted excellent aspects of their teaching that could be used as evidence to support promotion or award applications. However, time and support to consider, collate and present evidence of excellence appropriate to their career stage can be valuable in achieving recognition, and in professional identity formation (Fanghanel, 2007, 2012, Gunn & Fisk, 2013; Quinlan, 2014). The *Promoting Teaching* project (HEA, 2013a, 2013b) was commissioned to provide benchmarking resources for institutions seeking to review and develop their promotion practices and procedures for teaching-focused academic careers. A further timely outcome of the project was the production of a guide, Making Evidence Count (HEA, 2013a). The benchmarking tools and the evidence guide were primarily intended to support those making judgements about promotions cases, and individuals seeking to articulate excellence in their award and promotion applications. The resources have, however, also proved to be useful in professional development activities for promotion committees, heads of department and schools, and other leaders and mentors. They can be used to engage with and debate on notions of excellence and to support the review of the criteria on which they determine the reward or recognition of excellence (McHanwell & Robson, 2017). The intention is not that these resources should be regarded as definitive criteria for assessing teaching quality, but that they can be used to stimulate dialogue and encourage review of the breadth of evidence from a wide scope of activity that is considered important to cases of teaching excellence. The resources encompass threshold expectations for student-facing work, such as student engagement and curriculum development, which are already key elements of accredited training and development offerings. They also encompass leadership and collaboration, research and scholarship, and professional learning. These perhaps less consistently recognised forms of excellence are therefore discussed in turn.

LEADERSHIP AND COLLABORATION

Leaders have key roles to play in relation to learning and teaching development. Yet there is a scant literature on leadership of teaching (Marshall, Orell, Cameron, Bosanquet, & Thomas, 2011; Quinlan, 2014). Hofmeyer, Sheingold,

Klopper, and Warland (2015, p. 182) offer useful distinctions between 'leadership as position; leadership as performance; leadership as practice; and leadership as professional role model'.

Leadership at programme level, to oversee the design and delivery of the curriculum, to monitor the teaching and assessment methods employed, and the quality of the student experience, is generally recognised as an important and largely managerial position that contributes towards the achievement of excellent learning outcomes for students (Robson, 2015). Professional training for module leaders and programme leaders is routinely offered in many institutions. More senior teaching-focused leadership positions, for example the role of Dean of Undergraduate or Postgraduate Studies, also tend to involve the more managerial and quality assurance aspects of teaching. This reflects the conceptual ambiguity around the terms 'leading' and 'managing' (Marshall et al., 2011) underpinning the official designation of teaching-focused positions.

Recognition of a range of forms of teaching leadership is variable and promotion for leaders of teaching, particularly to the higher levels of Reader/Associate Professor and Chair, is uneven across the sector (Behari-Leak, 2017; Cashmore et al., 2013; Fung & Gordon, 2016; Gunn & Fisk, 2013; Quinlan, 2014). More nuanced understandings of excellence in leadership are needed to acknowledge leaders' contributions to the promotion of a quality culture around teaching (Bendermacher, noude Engbrink, Wolfhagen, & Dolmans, 2016; Blackmore et al., 2016). Teaching leaders who influence organisational processes, act as professional role models to other aspiring leaders and shape the socio-cultural environment of the campus (Quinlan, 2014) facilitate a critical dialogue around learning and teaching that is vital to culture change. Creating a collaborative culture in which teachers engage in critical dialogue about learning and teaching helps to develop a sense of agency, and a sense of connection in their contribution to teaching excellence (Van Lankveld et al., 2016).

Recognition of more democratic and less hierarchical models of leadership is increasing, as a means to develop leadership capacity in teaching and a sense of collective responsibility for changing HE cultures (Bolden, Jones, David, & Gentle, 2015; Quinlan, 2014). Ensuring that appropriate mentoring and support for professional learning is available to teaching-focused colleagues is important as they navigate the personal and professional, structural and cultural challenges that they may encounter as they construct their professional roles and identities (Behari-Leak, 2017).

The ability to demonstrate a wide sphere of influence, and contribution to the review and development of policies and practices at one's own and other institutions, locally, nationally and internationally, evidenced through publications and participation at conferences or in other professional fora, is important to senior teaching leadership development. Excellence in educational leadership at this level can facilitate transformations in policy and practice (Fung et al., 2017) that attract national and international recognition, and should be rewarded in comparable ways to research excellence.

RESEARCH AND SCHOLARSHIP

Leadership at senior level requires parity of opportunity in terms of time for research, scholarship and collaborative engagement with peers, which many academics regard as preferred forms of professional development, enabling them to provide the evidence of 'valued contributions to the academy', such as publications and awards, that are often required in promotions criteria (Locke et al., 2016, p. 77).

However, time for research and scholarship is important at all career stages. Knowledge about learning and teaching can be constructed through formal research, collaborative enquiry, engaging with the literature and through practice and experimentation (Mentkowski et al., 2000, cited in Kreber, 2002, p. 9). Whereas 'training' programmes for university teachers are often criticised for inherent weaknesses, including concerns about the relevance and transferability of content and methods for different disciplinary contexts (Fanghanel, 2012); time to engage in research and scholarship, as identified earlier in this chapter, is a key concern for many teaching-focused academics. Research and scholarly activity are often regarded as the most valuable forms of professional development, not only for those seeking job security and promotion (Locke et al., 2016; Robson, Wall, & Lofthouse, 2013) but also for those wishing to enhance their professional learning. For colleagues with more student-facing roles, scholarly leave or sabbaticals to develop textbooks, course materials or e-learning resources, or, for those engaged in vocational subjects, to refresh their experience as practitioners in their professions, can benefit the individual, their institution and the students (Locke et al., *ibid.*).

PROFESSIONAL LEARNING

Opportunity to engage in collaborative enquiry with colleagues across disciplines and institutions, professional bodies and special interest groups, associations and committees, can be a highly valued and productive form of professional learning for teachers at all levels. In the global knowledge economy, access to international networks and communities provides increasingly valuable professional learning fora (Guruz, 2011). Technological advances make virtual connections possible; and collaborations are facilitated when members share a common language, a common focus and a capacity to work in intercultural environments (*ibid.*, p. 19).

Socially oriented, participatory paradigms of professional learning can contribute to active and dynamic identity formation and renegotiation through different forms of participation (Jawitz, 2009; Stibbe, 2010–2011; Vandamme, 2014), supported by critical self-reflection and social recognition (Gu, 2011).

Networks for collaborative enquiry, drawing on action research and action leadership models, can provide professional learning in participatory, non-hierarchical, democratic, ethical and inclusive ways (Quinlan, 2014; Zuber-Skerritt, Fletcher, & Kearney, 2015). They provide fora for dialogue, opportunities to share practices and beliefs, and to critically engage with relevant literature, methodologies and partnerships for research. Expertise is developed through authentic and theorised approaches to teaching, as a process, or as a product, of ethical enquiry (Gregory & Gregory, 2013; Jawitz, 2009; Kreber, 2002; Robson et al., 2013).

Comparison of practices can be productive within such networks. Robson et al. (2013) note the compelling evidence to suggest that teacher learning is enhanced in collaborative settings, where practices involve critical reflectivity and scrutiny and critique by peers (Andresen, 2000; Cordingley, Bell, Evans, & Firth, 2005, cited in Robson et al., 2013). Their methodology for systematic, collaborative inquiry into teaching and learning practices not only provides a structure in which the epistemological and pedagogical foundations and rationales for practice can be discussed and developed, but also rigour through sharing the outcomes of the inquiry for public critique (Stenhouse, 1981, cited in Robson et al., 2013). Inquiry networks of this kind can support colleagues to consider the structures, policies and environments in which their teaching is located and to identify how departmental, faculty, university, national and international agendas shape their identity (Fanghanel, 2007). Systematic inquiry into teaching can provide rich data to challenge negative perceptions of practice knowledge (Hammersley, 2010, cited in Robson et al., 2013) and to demonstrate the impact on learning outcomes and the student experience of the theorised practices employed by excellent teachers.

Networks for collaborative enquiry, based upon more democratic notions of teaching excellence, can promote interactional leadership, in which different members provide leadership in response to particular situations, tasks and decisions, regardless of their roles (Knight & Trowler, 2000). Expert guidance from network members can give communicative power and legitimacy to the ideas and practices that develop (Robson et al. 2013; Zuber-Skerritt et al., 2015). The network can provide the productive conditions for development sought by many teaching-focused academics, through professional learning as participation (Wenger, 1998). This helps to explain how practices evolve, and identities are developed and transformed as members provide interpretive support for others in their communities of practice (*ibid.*). As network members explore and reflect on their work, engage with each other and with the literature, ideas are interpreted and reinterpreted and more theorised or principled accounts of teaching are constructed (Light, Calkins, & Cox, 2011; Sadler, Selkrig, & Manathunga, 2017; Zuber-Skerritt et al., 2015), contributing to the quality culture in their institutions (Fung et al., 2017).

Although the literature on HE has revealed a lack of consensus in conceptualisations of university teaching excellence, looking to the broader educational research literature, James and Pollard (2011) outline useful, evidence-informed generic principles for effective teaching and learning drawn from 10 years of research in the Teaching and Learning Research Programme (TLRP). With the aim to improve outcomes for students of all ages, the principles are grouped under four main themes: educational values and purposes; curriculum, pedagogy and assessment; personal and social processes and relationships; and teachers and policies (*ibid.*).

James and Pollard (2011) note a key principle relating to teaching policies, that effective pedagogies for HE depend on the learning of all those who support the learning of others (James & Pollard, ibid, p. 9). Developing teacher excellence through practice-based inquiry, involving practice and experimentation (Mentkowski et al., 2000), is especially highlighted.

CONCLUDING DISCUSSION

This chapter has taken a critical perspective on discourses of 'excellence' in HE teaching. It has reflected on the extent to which academic work has changed in recent decades, with the massification of HE and the increasing demands placed upon universities by national governments and external agencies. The quest for quality reflects and responds to the academic, social, economic and political challenges facing HE institutions as discussed in Chapter 2. The market pressures facing the sector suggest that it is timely for universities to think beyond their reputation for research excellence and to celebrate teaching excellence, not only as a means to improve their market position and competitiveness, but also as a means to attract, develop and retain excellent teachers.

Coates and Goedegebuure (2012) suggest that universities may need to consider their capacity to respond to the demands of the global student market. A review of selection, promotion and professional development procedures may be timely to ensure that prevailing conceptualisations of academic work reflect the reality of the modern academic role. 'There is an overarching need to consider the evolving nature of academic roles and for a fresh conceptualisation of academic work that is authentic and feasible' (*ibid*., p. 875). The academic career structure should enable teaching excellence in all its forms to be developed and nurtured, recognised and celebrated.

Turning to the contentious issue of quality measures and teaching excellence: is it possible to design effective systems to both measure *and* improve the quality of learning and teaching in HE? Research carried out in the school sector suggests that student progress is the yardstick by which teacher quality should be assessed (Coe, Aloisi, Higgins, & Major, 2014; James & Pollard, 2011). TEF metrics can provide broad indications of quality in terms of evidence of student progress and student satisfaction, but they fail to tell the whole story about teaching excellence. The contribution to excellence of education leaders, of teachers with sophisticated, research-informed professional beliefs and identities, pedagogies and practices, and of innovative, collaborative networks and teaching teams, require more nuanced definitions of excellence, and differentiated forms of support and development.

This chapter has attempted to contribute to thinking about what more nuanced and comprehensive understandings of teaching excellence might involve and how HE institutions and quality agencies might enable these more complex forms of evidence to be developed, presented, recognised and rewarded, to reflect the full range of teaching excellence across the academic career. It argues that a reframing of notions of teaching excellence in some institutions may be necessary to enable more sophisticated understandings of excellence to be communicated, debated and deployed to create a quality culture around teaching.

To add to the challenge for TEF, evidence of excellence is highly variable across institutions, faculties, and disciplines, cultures and contexts, because of differences in national and institutional missions and discourses. It is therefore difficult to envisage a single common measure of teaching excellence. A range of structural, social and cultural factors influence the positions from which teachers reflect on and theorise their practice (Lesnick, 2005) in the messy reality of the modern academic role (Debowski, 2012).

Strong and innovative arrangements for professional learning are strategically important to enhance the quality and relevance of learning and teaching in HE (Barnes et al., 1994). While each HEI will face specific economic and cultural challenges, the overall aim for HE teaching across the sector is strikingly similar – to ensure the quality of student learning. A greater emphasis on teacher professional learning is crucial to develop effective pedagogies for all those who support the learning of others in HE (James & Pollard, 2011). Professional learning through enquiry-based, interdisciplinary, inter-institutional and intercultural collaborations, networks and dialogue will help to ensure that the sector has the capacity to meet market demands with teaching that is theorised, evidence-based, principled, culturally responsive and inclusive. Further debate and dialogue would be welcome to consider the ways in which teaching excellence can become a priority for the HE sector in the ways that HERB outlines.

REFERENCES

Andresen, L. W. (2000). A usable, trans-disciplinary conception of scholarship. *Higher Education Research and Development*, *19*(2), 137–153.

Australian Learning and Teaching Council. (2009). Peer review of teaching for promotion purposes a project to develop and implement a pilot program of external peer review of teaching at four Australian universities. Final Project Report June 2009. Retrieved from http://www.adelaide.edu.au/teaching-projects/peerreview/peerReviewReport_part1.pdf

Barnes, J., Berendt, B., Csirik, J., El Hares, H., ter Haar, G., Jones, J., … Vessuri, H. (1994). Higher education staff development: Directions for the 21st century. Paris, United Nations Educational, Scientific and Cultural Organisation.

Baumfield, V., Hall, E., Higgins, S., & Wall, K. (2009). Catalytic tools: Understanding the interaction of inquiry and feedback in teachers' learning. *European Journal of Teacher Education*, *32*(4), 423–435.

Beckmann, E. A. (2016). Teaching excellence: recognising the many as well as the few. Retrieved from http://herdsa2016.org/images/188_Beckmann__RefPaper.pdf

Behari-Leak, K. (2017). New academics, new higher education contexts: A critical perspective on professional development. *Teaching in Higher Education*. doi:10.1080/13562517.2016.273215

Bendermacher, G. W. G., noude Engbrink, M. G. A., Wolfhagen, I. H. A. P., & Dolmans, D. H. J. M. (2016). Unravelling quality culture in higher education: A realist view. *Higher Education*. doi:10.1080/03075079.2012.754855

Blackmore, P., Blackwell, R., & Edmondson, M. (2016). *Tackling wicked issues: Prestige and employment outcomes in the teaching excellence framework*. HEPI Occasional Paper. Retrieved from www.hepi.ac.uk

Bolden, R., Jones, S., David, H., & Gentle, P. (2015). *Developing and leading shared leadership in higher education*. Stimulus Paper. London, Leadership Foundation for Higher Education.

Bråten, H. (2014). Searching for the Holy Grail - Excellence in teaching and learning in Norway. A study of Centres of Excellence in Education (SFUs). Paper presented in track 3 at the EAIR 36th Annual Forum in Essen, Germany, 27–30 August 2014.

Brew, A. (2012). Teaching and research: New relationships and their implications for inquiry-based teaching and learning in higher education. *Higher Education Research and Development*, *31*(1).

Brusoni, M., Damian, R., Sauri, J. G., Jackson, S., Kömürcügil, H., Malmedy, M., … Zobel, L. (2014). *The concept of excellence in higher education. European Association for Quality Assurance in Higher Education*. AISBL 2014, Brussels. Occasional Papers 20.

Burke, P. J., Stevenson, J., & Whelan, P. (2015). Teaching 'Excellence' and pedagogic stratification in higher education. *International Studies in Widening Participation*, *2*(2), 29–43.

Cashmore, A., & Ramsden, P. (2009a). *Reward and recognition of teaching in higher education: A collaborative investigation. Interim Report*. York: Higher Education Academy.

Cashmore, A., & Ramsden, P. (2009b). *Reward and recognition in higher education: Institutional policies and their implementation*. York: Higher Education Academy.

Cashmore, A., Cane, C., Cane, R., & Stainton, C. (2013). *Rebalancing promotion in the HE sector: Is teaching excellence being rewarded?* York: Higher Education Academy.

Clifford, V., & Montgomery, C. (2014). Challenging conceptions of Western Higher Education and developing graduates as global citizens. *Higher Education Quarterly*, *68*(1), 28–45. doi:10.1111/hequ.12029

Coates, H., & Goedegebuure, L. (2012). Recasting the academic workforce: Why the attractiveness of the academic profession needs to be increased and eight possible strategies for how to go about this from an Australian perspective. *Higher Education*, *64*, 875–889. doi:10.1007/s10734-012-9534-3

Coe, R., Aloisi, C., Higgins, S., & Major, L. E. (2014). What makes great teaching? Review of the underpinning research. *The Sutton Trust*. Retrieved from www.suttontrust.com/.../10/What-makes-great-teaching-FINAL-4.11.14

Cordingley, P., Bell, M., Evans, D., & Firth, A. (2005). *The impact of collaborative CPD on classroom teaching and learning: What do teacher impact data tell us about collaborative CPD?* London: EPPI-Centre.

Debowski, S. (2012). *The new academic*. Berkshire: Open University Press.

Deem, R. (2015). *A critical commentary on Ray Land and George Gordon 'Teaching Excellence initiatives: Modalities and operational factors'*. York: Higher Education Academy.

Deem, R., Hillyard, S., & Reed, M. (2007). *Higher education and the new managerialism: The changing management of UK universities*. Oxford: Oxford University Press.

Deutsche Forschungsgemeinschaft (DFG). (2013). *The excellence initiative at a glance*. Retrieved from http://www.dfg.de/download/pdf/dfg_im_profil/geschaeftsstelle/publikationen/exin_broschuere_en.pdf

Dittrich, K. (2014). Preface: The significance of 'excellence'. In M. Brusoni, R. Damian, J. G. Sauri, S. Jackson, H. Kömürcügil, M. Malmedy, ...L. Zobel (Eds.), *The concept of excellence in higher education. European Association for Quality Assurance in Higher Education. AISBL 2014* (pp. 5–6). Brussels. Occasional Papers 20.

Enders, J., & de Weert, E. (Eds.). (2009). *The changing face of academic life – Analytical and comparative perspectives*. Basingstoke: Palgrave Macmillan.

Fanghanel, J. (2007). *Investigating university lecturers' pedagogical constructs in the working context*. The Higher Education Academy – January 2007. Retrieved from https://www.heacademy.ac.uk/system/files/fanghanel.pdf. Accessed on April 3, 2017.

Fanghanel, J. (2012). *Being an academic*. London: Routledge.

Forstenzer, J. (2016). *The teaching excellence framework: What's the purpose*? University of Sheffield, The Sir Bernard Crick Centre for Engaged Philosophy.

Fung, D., & Gordon, C. (2016, January 13). *Rewarding educators and education leaders*. York, Higher Education Academy.

Fung, D., Besters-Dilger, J., & van der Vaart, R., (2017, February). *Excellent education in research-intensive universities*. Belgium: League of European Research Universities (LERU).

Gibbs, G. (2016). Teaching. In *Higher Education Policy Institute response to the higher education green paper* (pp. 11–27). Oxford: HEPI.

Greatbatch, D., & Holland, J. (2016, May). *Teaching quality in higher education: Literature Review and Qualitative Research*. Department for Business, Innovation and Skills.

Gregory, M., & Gregory, M. V. (Eds.). (2013). *Teaching excellence in higher education*. Palgrave MacMillan.

Gu, M. M. (2011). The ethical formation of teacher identity: Pre-service teachers in Hong Kong. In M. L. C. Radhika Jaidev, W. J. Sadorra, L. M. Onn, & B. P. L. Cherk (Eds.), *Global perspectives, local initiatives: Reflections and practices in ELT* (pp. 183–195). Centre for English Language Communication, National University of Singapore.

Gunn, V., & Fisk, A. (2013). *Considering teaching excellence in higher education 2007-2013: A literature review since the CHERI Report 2007*. York: Higher Education Academy.

Guruz, K. (2011). *Higher education and international student mobility in the global knowledge economy*. Albany, NY: State University of New York Press.

Hammersley, M. (2010, July). Think piece: Unreflective practice? Case study and the problem of theoretical inference. Keynote presented at the Higher Education Close Up 5 Conference, Lancaster, UK. Retrieved from www.lancs.ac.uk/fss/events/hecu5/docs/Hammersley. Accessed on April 3, 2017.

Hénard, F. (2010). *Learning our lesson. Review of quality teaching in higher education institutional management in higher education*. OECD. ISBN: 9264079270.

Higher Education Academy. (2013a). *Making evidence count*. Retrieved from https://www.heacademy.ac.uk/resources/detail/recognition/making-evidence-count-web. Accessed on October 27, 2016.

Higher Education Academy. (2013b). *Promoting teaching: International inter-university benchmarking of academic promotion*. Final Report. University of Leicester, Newcastle University, University of Tasmania, University of Wollongong.

Higher Education Academy. (2017). HEA global teaching excellence awards. Retrieved from https://www.heacademy.ac.uk/about/news/hea-global-teaching-excellence-awards. Accessed on April 24, 2017.

Higher Education Funding Council for England. (2017). *The teaching excellence framework TEF*. Retrieved from http://www.hefce.ac.uk/lt/tef/.

Hill, L. *Leadership development: A strategic imperative for higher education*. Retrieved from https://net.educause.edu/ir/library/pdf/ffp0506s.pdf

Hofmeyer, A., Sheingold, B. H., Klopper, H. C., & Warland, J. (2015). Leadership in learning and teaching in higher education: Perspectives of academics in non-formal leadership roles. *Contemporary Issues in Education Research, Third Quarter 2015*, *8*(3), 181–192.

James, M., & Pollard, A. (2011). TLRP's ten principles for effective pedagogy: Rationale, development, evidence, argument and impact. *Research Papers in Education*, *26*(3), 275–328.

Jarboe, N. (2016). Women count: Leaders in higher education 2016. *Women Count*. Retrieved from https://womencountblog.files.wordpress.com/2016/04/women-count-report_web_final.pdf

Jawitz, J. (2009). Academic identities and communities of practice in a professional discipline. *Teaching in Higher Education*, *14*(3), 241–251. doi:10.1080/14748460701661260.

Knight, P. T., & Trowler, P. R. (2000). Department-level cultures and the improvement of learning and teaching. *Studies in Higher Education*, *25*(1), 69–83, doi:10.1080/030750700116028

Kreber, C. (2002). Teaching excellence, teaching expertise and the scholarship of teaching. *Innovative Higher Education*, *27*(1), 5–23. Fall 2002.

Land, R., & Gordon, G. (2015). *Teaching excellence initiatives: Modalities and operational factors*. Higher Education Academy.

Law, S. (2011). *Recognising excellence in teaching and learning. Report from the consultation on the UKPSF professional standards framework for teaching and supporting learning in higher education*. York: Higher Education Academy.

Leask, B. (2009). Using formal and informal curricula to improve interactions between home and international students. *Journal of Studies in International Education*, *13*(2), 205–221. doi:10.1177/1028315308329786

Leibowitz, B., Farmer, J., & Franklin, J. (2012). Teaching excellence awards in South Africa – A national study. *Higher Education Monitor* 13.

Lesnick, A. (2005). The mirror in motion: Redefining reflective practice in an undergraduate fieldwork seminar. *Reflective Practice*, 6(1), 33–48, doi:10.1080/1462394042000326798

Light, G., Calkins, S., & Cox, R. (2011). *Learning and teaching in higher education: The reflective professional*. London: Sage.

Locke, W., Whitchurch, C., Smith, H. J., & Mazenod, A. (2016). *Shifting landscapes: Meeting the staff development needs of the changing academic workforce*. York: The Higher Education Academy.

MacKenzie, J., & Robertson, A. (2009). Teaching excellence Awards in Scottish higher education. *Practice and evidence of scholarship of teaching and learning in higher education*, 4(1), 26–40.

Mak, A. S., Daly, A., & Barker, M. C. (2014). Fostering cultural inclusiveness and learning in culturally mixed business classes. *Springerplus. 2014*, 3, 242. doi:10.1186/2193-1801-3-242

Marshall, S. J., Orrell, J., Cameron, A., Bosanquet, A., & Thomas, S. (2011). Leading and managing learning and teaching in higher education. *Higher Education Research and Development*, *30*(2), 87–103.

McAleese, M. (2013, June). *High level group on the modernisation of higher education*. Report to the European Commission on Improving the quality of teaching and learning in Europe's higher education institutions (pp. 6–7). Luxembourg: Publications Office of the European Union.

McHanwell, S., & Robson, S. (2017, April 11). Dimensions of teaching excellence: Recognising and rewarding teaching excellence in higher education institutions. Plenary presentation, Association of National Teaching Fellows Annual Symposium, Aston University, Manchester.

Mentkowski, M., & Associates. (2000). *Learning that lasts*. San Francisco, CA: Jossey-Bass.

OECD Innovation Strategy. (2015). An agenda for policy action. Retrieved from https://www.oecd.org/innovation/OECD-Innovation-Strategy-2015-CMIN2015-7.pdf. Accessed on January 15, 2017.

Probert, B. (2013). *Teaching-focused academic appointments in Australian universities: Recognition, specialisation or stratification?* Sydney: Office for Learning and Teaching.

Pruvot, E. B., & Estermann, T. (2014). *DEFINE Thematic Report: Funding for Excellence*. Brussels: European University Association.

Quinlan, K. M. (2014). Leadership of teaching for student learning in higher education: What is needed? *Higher Education Research and Development*, *33*(1), 32–45. doi:10.1080/07294360.2013.864609

Reid, S., & Spencer Oatey, H. (2013). Towards a global citizen: Utilising a competency framework to promote intercultural knowledge and skills in higher education students. In J. Ryan (Ed.), *Cross cultural teaching and learning for home and international students* (pp. 125–141). London: Routledge.

Robson, S. (2015). Internationalisation of the curriculum: Meanings, motives and methods. *Journal of Perspectives in Applied Academic Practice*, *3*(3). doi:10.14297/jpaap.v313.176

Robson, S., Wall, K., & Lofthouse, R. (2013). Raising the profile of innovative teaching in higher education? Reflections on the EquATE project. *International Journal of Teaching and Learning in Higher Education*, *25*(1), 92–102.

Sadler, K., Selkrig, M., & Manathunga, C. (2017). Teaching is … opening up spaces to explore academic work in fluid and volatile times. *Higher Education Research and Development*, *36*(1), 171–186. doi:10.1080/07294360.2016.1171299

Schindler, L., Puls-Elvidge, S., Welzant, H., & Crawford, L. (2015). Definitions of quality in higher education: A synthesis of the literature. *Higher Learning Research Communications*, *5*(3), 3–13. doi:10.18870/hlrc.v5i3.244

Searle, R., & McKenna, S. (2013). Teaching excellence in a transforming South Africa. In A. Skelton (Ed.), *International perspectives on teaching excellence*. Abingdon: Routledge.

Skelton, A. (2004). Understanding teaching excellence in higher education: A critical evaluation of the national teaching fellowships scheme. *Studies in Higher Education*, *29*(4), 451–468.

Standards and guidelines for quality assurance in the European higher education area. (2015). Brussels, Belgium.

Stenhouse, L. (1981). What counts as research? *British Journal of Educational Studies*, *29*(2), 103–114.

Stevenson, J., Burke, P.-J., & Whelan, P. (2014). *Pedagogic stratification and the shifting landscape of higher education* (pp. 1–48). York: Higher Education Academy.

Stibbe, A. (2010–2011). Identity reflection: Students and societies in transition. *Learning and Teaching in Higher Education*, *5*, 86–95.

van Lankveld, T., Schoonenboom, J., Volman, M., Croiset, G., & Beishuizen, J. (2016). Developing a teacher identity in the university context: A systematic review of the literature. *Higher Education Research and Development*. doi:10.1080/07294360.2016.1208154

Vandamme, R. C. (2014). How teachers construct their identity in higher professional education: A grounded theory study based on dialogical self theory and pattern language. Doctoral thesis. Retrieved from https://pure.uvt.nl/portal/en/publications/how-teachers-construct-their-identity-in-higher-professional-education(168eda7f-9309-4f81-8fa0-c11be269d32b).html

Vernos, I. (2013). Research management: Quotas are questionable. *Nature*, *495*, 39. doi:10.1038/495039a

Weir, A. (2009). Assuring quality in higher education: The New Zealand experience. *Journal of Institutional Research*, *14*(2), 60–72.

Wenger, E. (1998). *Communities of practice learning, meaning, and identity*. Cambridge: Cambridge University Press.

Wills, S. (2010). Teachers DO get promoted. Paper presented at the HEA National Teaching Fellows, University of Westminster, London.

Zuber-Skerritt, O., Fletcher, M., & Kearney, J. (2015). *Professional learning in higher education and communities: Towards a new vision for action research*. London: Palgrave Macmillan.

6

CONCLUSION

Amanda French and Matt O'Leary

This book has begun to explore why, given the conceptual problems of 'teaching excellence', has it not only persisted, but also become ubiquitous, not only for describing 'good' activities and institutions, and hopeful aspirations, but also in terms of high-quality teaching in higher education. The rise of metrics in education generally gives one possible reason for the persistence of this trend, which the Teaching Excellence Framework will only serve to intensify. However, over the development of this trend we have forgotten to ask whether what we are measuring is telling us anything useful about the processes that lie at the core of teaching. As Biesta argues (2017):

> *We have reached a situation where measurement is to a large degree driving education policy and practice without any longer asking whether what is being measured adequately represents a view of good education. (p. 316)*

As Stephen Ball (2007, p. 191) suggests, 'we need to move beyond the tyrannies of improvement, efficiency and standards, to recover a language of and for education articulated in terms of ethics, moral obligations and values'. As part of any such movement beyond improvement, discussions and work around teaching excellence need to move beyond the obsession with summative assessment and seek to strike a balance between the formative and summative. In doing so, HEIs need to create approaches that attempt to capture the complexity of learning and teaching in a much more sophisticated and authentic way by drawing on multiple sources of evidence as part of a multivariate framework.

In order to develop a rounded and credible picture of 'authentic' and 'effective' teaching as opposed to 'teaching excellence', a multidimensional range of sources of data and/or evidence need to be gathered. In order for this multidimensional range of evidence to be meaningful and to reflect the complexities of learning and teaching, a longitudinal perspective over time is needed rather than a snapshot or episodic perspective. This applies to both staff and students. In the case of the latter, this might involve tracking the journeys of students post-completion in order to gauge the value of their studies in a workplace context and how the knowledge and skills acquired during their studies have equipped them in their professional contexts. Piecing together a longitudinal view is certainly a significant challenge for any institution in terms of capturing and distilling this into a coherent and representative narrative, but it is a challenge worth pursuing if the institution is to ensure that the story it tells of the shared learning and teaching experiences of staff and students is authentic.

Whatever one's views about the TEF and whether it represents a forward or retrograde step for HE in the United Kingdom, it cannot be denied that it has generated a lot of discussion and debate about the practice of teaching in academia, its relationship with research and indeed its comparative status. That such discussions should be happening amongst academics within and across institutions is a step forward in itself. For too long learning and teaching have occupied a peripheral position in the sector strategically and operationally. TEF or no TEF, it's time that learning and teaching became a bigger priority in higher education.

REFERENCES

Ball, S. J. (2007). *Education plc: Understanding private sector participation in public sector education*. London: Routledge.

Biesta. (2017). Education, measurement and the professions: Reclaiming a space for democratic professionality in education. *Educational Philosophy and Theory*, *49*(4), 315–330.

INDEX